Apostolic ATHLETES

11 Priests and Bishops Reveal How Sports Helped Them Follow Christ's Call

Collected by Trent Beattie

Available from:
Marian Helpers Center
Stockbridge, MA 01263

Orderline: 1-800-462-7426
Website: marian.org

Publication Date:
April 15, 2018

Imprimi Potest:
Very Rev. Kazimierz Chwalek, MIC
Provincial Superior
The Blessed Virgin Mary, Mother of Mercy Province
June 23, 2017

Nihil Obstat:
Dr. Robert A. Stackpole, STD
Censor Deputatus
June 23, 2017

Library of Congress Catalog Number: 2017915448

ISBN: 978-1-59614-414-9

Cover images: © fotolia.com

MARIAN PRESS
STOCKBRIDGE MA 01263

Printed in the United States of America
2018

This book is dedicated to Brian Bergkamp (1992-2016), former seminarian for the Diocese of Wichita, Kansas. Brian was kayaking in the Arkansas River when a woman fell out of her kayak into the rushing waters. He saved her life at the expense of his own.

Brian demonstrated, in the context of an athletic/recreational setting, the self-sacrifice that is supposed to characterize the life of a priest. As Bishop Carl Kemme stated at Brian's funeral, "He may not have been a priest, but he lived and died a most priestly life."

Contents

FOREWORD

IN THE BOOK YOU HOLD IN YOUR HANDS, Trent Beattie has brought together the witnesses of 11 priests and bishops to the importance of sports in their lives. It is an inspiring read, whether you are an athlete, a spectator, or simply if you are trying to better understand someone in your life who has a passion for sports of any kind. These men of God he introduces us to share how their lives as athletes helped form them as men and, in some way, led them to stand *in persona Christi*, in the person of Christ, as they do today through the Sacrament of Holy Orders.

I know their journey well. I've traveled that road myself. I know about victory, and I know about defeat. I have, in some form or other, been involved in sports almost my entire life. I started baseball in kindergarten, wrestling in third grade, and football in sixth grade. In my sophomore year at Monroe Catholic Central High School in Monroe, Michigan, we never lost a football game, and I never lost a wrestling match. Now, that was a good thing — after all, who *wants* to lose? But it was also a bad thing. After a while, you start to feel you're invincible, that you alone are responsible for your success. You forget about luck. You forget about Providence, and that everything you have and everything you are is a gift from God, who holds you in existence with love.

But in Monroe, we didn't keep winning forever. In my junior year, we had a subpar football season *and* a bad wrestling season. Looking back, I recall how bewildering it was to me at the time: How was it that things could go so well one moment and so disastrously the next? I see so clearly now that the Lord was with me in defeat. He was with me as I limped back to that somber locker room, my head held low, after another bitter football loss. Defeat that year was a gift from God. By allowing me to experience a taste of failure, He was teaching me humility. He was forcing me to take a more critical and *healthier* look at myself and the world around me. He was preparing me for my true calling — the priesthood — to work with others who are down, who feel defeated, who yearn for victory, who need to know that God seeks to do great things through each and every one of us. Having suffered defeat myself, I'm better able to help others get back on their feet and into the game of life again.

Through sports (and throughout life), God sometimes allows us to be broken down before He builds us back up. We see this in the Bible, repeatedly — most famously in the story of a fellow wrestler, Jacob (see Gen 32:25-31). Like Jacob, we need to lose our wrestling matches with God. He needs to win in our hearts, our minds, and our lives. That's the secret of the Christian life: We must die to ourselves in order to win.

As you will see in this book, sports teach us other ways to die to self, as well, through the suffering involved in training, in working out, in getting up early for practice and spending all day on the field or the mat. I've died to self by fasting and sweating to make weight for wrestling. (In fact, I've missed many Thanksgiving dinners because of it.) I died to self every time my coach called me out for giving less than my best in practice, pointing out areas I needed to work on. Sports are all about dying to self for the team, for victory, for a greater good.

One example of this from my life as a Marian comes from one of the greatest grudge matches in the history of sports: the Dominican students and priests versus the Marian Fathers' students and priests at the Dominican House of Studies in Washington, D.C. We've played an annual softball game together for 15 years now, and in those 15 years, we've beaten the Dominicans once. (In our defense, they've always had a lot of possible players to choose from. There are a lot of guys there.)

That one Marian victory came when I and one other Marian in formation decided that we were sick of getting beat. It was time for a change. It was time for victory.

We organized and ran drills over and over and over. We didn't just do batting practice and hit ground balls; we got into detailed game scenarios. "Okay, two runners on, one runner out, fly ball to deep center. What do you do? You're on base, what do you do if the ball's hit to left field? If you hit it to right field?" We drilled and we drilled and we drilled.

We won 21-9.

That's the only year we've beaten them. I strongly believe that it was a result of those practices. Just as we had to practice so hard to win that game, we have to practice virtue to be able to become holy. We cannot have lives of heroic virtue unless we practice the small virtues consistently. Isn't that what the spiritual life is, that, every day, we have to work a little better?

It was the only year we would practice at that level. And that was the only year we won.

Saint Paul knew that sports could teach Christians how to die to self through training to win, how to achieve the goal of Christian life, which is life in Christ on earth as it is in Heaven. He wrote:

> Do you not know that the runners in the stadium all run in the race, but only one wins the prize? Run so as to win. Every athlete exercises discipline in every way. They do it to win a perishable crown, but we an imperishable one. Thus I do not run aimlessly; I do not fight as if I were shadowboxing. No, I drive my body and train it, for fear that, after having preached to others, I myself should be disqualified — 1 Cor 9:24-27.

Indeed, we — you, me, all of us — are in the greatest grudge match of our lives against the evil of Satan and his team. Sporting matches help prepare us to do battle and win.

Now, I don't think it's mandatory for priests to play sports, but I think it's helpful. Sports show that we have to work with each other to accomplish a goal. If you don't block for your quarterback, he's going to get clobbered. If you don't run the right pattern as a receiver, your quarterback is going to miss you, and your team is not going to be successful. Your offense can score and you could win, or if your defense doesn't tighten up even though your offense is still good, you can still lose. Everybody has a part to play (see Rom 12:4-8; see also 1 Cor 12:12-21).

The priests and bishops who share their stories in this book have learned the importance of teamwork in the service of Christ, and share their wisdom and experience to help you better run your own race and win your own imperishable crown. Follow in their footsteps. Discern the will of the Lord for your life, no matter what vocation He may be calling you to, whether that vocation involves marriage, religious life, priesthood, or the single life. Learn from their examples of discipline leading to death to self, both through sports and through living the faith.

May Jesus, the Divine Mercy, bless you, and Mary Immaculate pray for you.

Fr. Chris Alar, MIC
"Father Joseph, MIC"
Director, Association of Marian Helpers

INTRODUCTION

Giving the Priesthood a Sporting Chance

SPORTS CAN BE GREAT SCHOOLS OF VIRTUE or great hindrances to virtue, depending on the way we decide to use them. Many good deeds (such as attending Mass on Sundays) are hindered when we see footballs and tennis rackets as being more important than the worship of God. However, many good deeds (such as passing along valuable life lessons to youth) can occur when we see sports for what they are meant to be: means for getting us closer to God.

I've been blessed to have conducted dozens of sports-related interviews with faithful Catholics, many of which are included in the book *Fit for Heaven* (Dynamic Catholic, 2015). Most of these interviews are with laymen, but all of the stories in the book you are now holding come from ordained priests who have gained — and continue to gain — spiritual strength through sports.

Soccer, football, and baseball seem to be the most popular sports with these athletic priests, but some of their testimonies include hockey, spear-fishing, and snowboarding. God calls ordinary men to become His ministers, so it should be no surprise that many of them have athletic backgrounds. However, there is still something attention-grabbing about priests and seminarians competing in sporting events such as the baseball games of the DC Padres in Maryland.

Father David Wells is a member of the DC Padres and a contributor to this book (see page 63). His experiences with baseball — both good and bad — helped to lead him toward the priesthood. Also instrumental were his experiences with his uncle, a priest. Many positives in their relationship were temporarily overshadowed by an enormous negative when his uncle was murdered, but not even this could prevent the grace of God from working in his life.

Father Wells proceeded toward the priesthood with the help of Mass, Confession, and the Divine Mercy Chaplet at the National Shrine of the Divine Mercy in Stockbridge, Massachusetts. Now he brings the merciful love of God the Father to his own parishioners in Gaithersburg, Maryland. He also finds time to play baseball — for fun, but also for promoting vocations to the priesthood, an integral part of the DC Padres' mission.

There are many other examples in this book of how sports serve as vehicles for something higher and more enduring. Rather than going down the road much of society takes with sports — that of idolatry — the men in this book use their athletic skills to lead souls in lives of sanctifying grace. This is the calling of all Christians, but most particularly of priests, the official ministers of the Church.

So grand is the importance of the priesthood that without it the Church would be ... well, it would not be the Church. As explained in the *Catechism of the Council of Trent*, the other Sacraments depend on the Sacrament of Holy Orders "to such an extent that without it, some of them could not be constituted or administered at all ... ."

Without the priesthood, there would be no Mass and no Confession, the most commonly received Sacraments. Souls would languish and wither away from lack of spiritual nourishment and renewal. Sanctifying grace would disappear from the earth and darkness would reign.

However, God has other plans. By the words of a priest, God comes down from Heaven in the Sacrifice of the Mass, and by the words of a priest, souls headed for hell are redirected to Heaven in the Sacrament of Confession. What more sublime profession could there be? The men in this book see that the highest work they could ever do is found in the priesthood, because the priesthood is a continuation of the life of Christ the High Priest.

Saint John Vianney, the patron of parish priests, wrote in the 1800s: "The priesthood is the love of the heart of Jesus. When you see the priest, think of Our Lord Jesus Christ." Although organized sports were not nearly as popular in 19th-century Europe as they are now, they were used by another saint from that time and continent to manifest the love of Christ. Saint John Bosco reached young people through games that were familiar to them. This started a progression from natural happiness to the happiness of Heaven and the beatific vision, the ultimate expression of God's love.

Clergymen of today have numerous opportunities to show God's love through sports. In this book, two bishops and nine priests share in their own words what sports have meant to them and their ministries. These ministers of God come from diverse backgrounds and are stationed in places from California to Massachusetts to engage in work for dioceses or orders. What they share with each other is the realization that sports can benefit mankind. Because we live in a sacramental world, something as mundane as a soccer ball can lead to something as sublime as service at the altar

Bishop Thomas Paprocki of Springfield, Illinois, leads the first group of priests, while Bishop John Barres of Rockville Centre, New York, leads the second group. Originally there were to be two groups of six ministers, giving us the apostolic number of 12. However, one of the contributors encountered some trouble — including a tornado — that prevented him from getting his chapter done in time.

This can be seen as a loss, but also a symbolic gain. Perhaps the missing "12th man" could be you or a man you know. After prayerfully reading the sporting stories in this book, you or a relative or a friend may be better equipped to contact a pastor, local vocations director, or even one of the men in this book to discuss things further. That way, the priesthood will be given a sporting chance.

Trent Beattie
January 31, 2017
Feast of St. John Bosco

BISHOP
THOMAS JOHN PAPROCKI

How Sports Made Me the
Bishop that I Am

THE FIRST THING THAT NEEDS TO BE SAID about how sports have played a role in my vocation is that I am not really a very talented athlete. I have learned as much, if not more, from my failures in sports as from my successes. Ask any of my brothers or schoolmates with whom I played sports as a boy, and they will most likely tell you that when we were picking sides for a game in whatever sport, I was usually among the last to be chosen. But I did find two sports that I loved and played well enough at least to have fun doing so: hockey and running.

I am the third of nine children, the oldest and youngest of whom are girls; the seven in the middle, boys. We always had plenty of people to play with, even in our own household. The sports we played together most often were hockey, baseball, and softball. The particular version of softball that we played was done with a ball 16 inches in circumference, but without using mitts. I was surprised to find out when I got older that the 16-inch softball is unique to the Chicago area!

Growing up on the South Side of Chicago, I was and still am a White Sox fan, even though that was not the case with all of my brothers. In fact, there was a pattern that might suggest a bit of sibling rivalry in the choice of our favorite baseball teams. My older brother, Jim, is a Cubs fan. I, the next in line, am a Sox fan. My next brother, Ed, is a Cubs fan. After Ed come the twins, John and Ron, who are both Sox fans. Next after the twins is Joe, who is a Cubs fan. My youngest brother, Allen, started out as a Sox fan but switched to the Cubs after the White Sox traded his favorite player, Harold Baines, for the second time. I thought perhaps after the Sox got Baines back for a third time in 2000 that Allen would return to the fold, but even the Sox winning the World Series in 2005 couldn't convince him to come back from "the Dark Side." So of the seven boys in our family, three have always been White Sox fans, three have always been Cubs fans, and one was first a Sox fan and then a Cubs fan! I guess that's fitting, since our dad, John H. Paprocki, Jr., always said he was neither a Sox fan nor a Cubs fan, but a Chicago fan.

When it came to professional hockey, there was only one team in town, and that was the Black Hawks (who later changed the spelling of the team name to "Blackhawks," even though they are named for Chief Black Hawk, who was a real person and after whom the 19th century Black Hawk War was named). I have some vivid memories of Dad from my childhood, especially of going to church with him and Mom, anything having to do with the family car (since I loved cars), and going to watch the Black Hawks at the old Chicago Stadium. It was a thrill just going with Dad to the box office in the afternoon to buy tickets, seeing the empty seats in the arena and the vacant ice, which later that day would be filled with fans and swarming with skaters swirling around the rink.

In the spring of 1961, when I was 8 years old, the Black Hawks won the Stanley Cup with two exciting young players named Bobby Hull and Stan Mikita. The White Sox had won the American League pennant just two years previously in 1959, so winning seemed like something I could expect from my favorite sports teams in the years to come. Little did I know that they would not achieve the pinnacle of success in their respective sports until the White Sox won the World Series in 2005 and the Blackhawks won the Stanley Cup in 2010, 2013, and 2015. In the meantime, there was a lot of failure and frustration for Chicago teams. There was so much failure and frustration that I wrote two of the eight chapters of my book, *Holy Goals for Body and Soul: Eight Steps to Connect Sports with God and Faith* (Ave Maria Press, 2013), on failure and frustration. I also wrote about fear and how our fears, especially our fear of failure, can be an obstacle to getting involved in the first place in sports or practically anything else in life.

We can respond to our fears, failures, and frustrations either by fleeing from them or striving to conquer them. I suggest five steps to overcoming our fears, failures, and frustrations: faith, fortitude, family, friendship, and fun. While all of these five steps can be helpful, just a couple of them — or even only one — can make the difference in conquering our fears, failures, and frustrations.

In hockey, for example, most people want nothing to do with playing goalie. They're not interested in standing in front of a net with someone shooting a hard rubber puck at them at speeds of up to 100 miles per hour. Most goalies will tell you that it is a fearsome experience, but getting hurt is not what goalies fear most. Over the years, I have had many injuries playing goalie, including knee surgery, a broken finger on my catching hand, and several stitches and scars on my face after being hit in the mask with the puck. As soon as I heal, however, I am ready to get back into the nets. So getting injured is not the primal fear. Giving up goals is what we fear most; in other words, we fear failure. Hockey goaltending is the only position in all of sports where a red light flashes and horns blare whenever the goalie makes a mistake. Imagine working at your desk at the office or taking an exam in school, and every time you made a mistake, a red light would flash and a foghorn would sound! Well, that's what goalies have to put up with (at least in the pros; fortunately, amateur hockey usually spares us goalies that indignity). But that's also why many very skilled athletes want nothing to do with playing goalie. You can either flee from the fear or confront it head-on.

This is true, not just in sports, but in other areas of life, as well. Surveys report that most people's biggest fear is not death. (That fear comes in at number two.) Most people's number one fear is public speaking. In other words, most people would literally rather die than get up in front of a group and give a speech. Why? For fear of failure, of making a mistake or publicly appearing foolish.

Fear of public speaking was an issue for me when I was in the seminary. Preaching a homily in front of a large congregation is something a priest has to do. My desire to be a priest goes back to my early childhood, as far back as I can remember. So I went to a high school seminary in Chicago, Quigley Preparatory Seminary South, to begin my studies for the priesthood at age 14. Since I was rather quiet and shy, the thought of getting up in front of people to preach was frightening, to say the least. In fact, my own experience of being afraid of public speaking leads me to believe that the requirement to preach in public is as much — if not more! — of an obstacle to considering a vocation to the priesthood as celibacy is.

So what did I do? Again, you can either flee from the fear or confront it head-on. My desire and my sense of being called by God to be a priest were so great that fleeing from my vocation was not an option. So I confronted my fear head-on. I took speech courses in the college seminary for the Archdiocese of Chicago, Niles College of Loyola University, and homiletics (how to preach homilies or sermons) in the major seminary at St. Mary of the Lake Seminary in Mundelein, Illinois. In my speech course in college, the professor initially gave us topics to talk about in front of the class. I struggled with those assignments at first, but my big breakthrough came when the professor told us that for our next speech, *we* could choose the topic and talk about anything we wanted. So naturally, I put on all of my goalie equipment and gave a "show and tell" speech about the art of goaltending in hockey. I found that I could talk with ease at great length about a subject so near and dear to my heart, so much so that the professor had to cut me off after about 20 minutes, saying, "I think we've heard enough about goaltending, Mr. Paprocki!" What I learned is that I could transfer that skill of talking about something near and dear to my heart to the life of faith. Public speaking still gives me a healthy nervous tension and an adrenaline rush that helps motivate me to pray and prepare, but talking about God and other matters of faith are not fearsome when they emerge from experiences of the heart.

A couple of other experiences from college also had a big impact on my vocation as a priest and as a bishop. When I was a freshman in college seminary, we had to take a physical fitness test that consisted of some running and performing a number of exercises. One of the exercises was to do chin-ups hanging from a chin-up bar. Looking up at the bar, I wasn't sure if I could even reach it. I don't recall for sure, but I may have even used a chair to help me up to the bar. Once I got my underhand grip on the bar, I hung there and discovered, to my utter dismay, that I could not lift my body to do even one chin-up. Not a single one: total failure. Well, my humiliation provided the motivation I needed. I determined to do something about it. I began practicing chin-ups until I could do 15 in a row. To this day, I have a chin-up bar in the doorway between my bedroom and the closet, and I do 15 chin-ups when I wake up in the morning.

My other key college experience also involved the same coach who conducted the physical fitness exam that I had so miserably failed. His name was Tom Kleeman. Coach Kleeman was the college's athletic director, coach of the junior varsity basketball team, golf coach, and coach of several other sports, in addition to teaching physical education. There was something about his enthusiastic demeanor and the compassionate way he treated those of us who were not the most gifted athletes that made me want to work with him. So I volunteered for the athletic committee, eventually becoming its chairman and the sports information director. In those capacities, I helped Coach Kleeman schedule and publicize the varsity sports, and I ran the whole intramural athletic program, consisting of basketball, touch football, volleyball, tennis, handball, ping-pong, and of course, my innovation to the program: floor hockey!

At Coach Kleeman's 85th birthday party in October of 2014, I publicly thanked him for helping me become the bishop I am today. He looked a bit puzzled that I would give so much credit to the sports program and him personally as such key components of my seminary formation, so I explained what I had learned from him: not only how to schedule and organize so many activities, but even more importantly, how to deal effectively and cheerfully with a wide variety of people and their various personalities, interests, skills, needs, and demands. Undoubtedly, his influence was favorably assisted by the fact that he started every gym class by leading us in praying the Hail Mary!

Later in life, the sport that would take on a greater amount of my time and energy was running — marathon running, to be specific. I was not on the track or cross-country team in high school, but I started running for the sake of my own health when I was a high school senior, after reading about the cardiovascular benefits of aerobic training. Since three of my grandparents had died in their 50s, all before I was born, I figured that with a gene pool like that, I had better start exercising if I wanted to live past 55.

I remember running my first mile. My high school did not have a track, but it was a quarter-mile around the parking lot. While running those four laps, my lungs were burning, my legs were weary, and my brain was screaming for me to stop. Again, rather than give up, I determined to overcome these hurdles. For the next few years, I rarely ran farther than one mile, but when I went to the major seminary at Mundelein, I started running around the lake on campus, which was three miles in circumference.

During my last year of seminary, I was assigned to a parish as a deacon, where I started running six to eight miles with some high school students from the local cross-country team. That remained my maximum mileage until I was in my 40s. During that span of years, marathon running had become more and more popular in the United States, but I had never had any interest in running a marathon until one day when I was with my brothers.

My brothers and I had just finished playing a game of floor hockey and went out for pizza. It was right after Christmas in December of 1994, and we were sitting around a table talking about New Year's resolutions. When it was my turn to announce my New Year's resolution, I just blurted out, "I'm thinking of doing a marathon next year." My youngest brother, Allen, was next, and he said, "That's funny! I'm thinking of running a marathon, too!" Well, within a few months, Allen and I were training for the 1995 Chicago Marathon.

In the course of my training, I decided that I would use my running of the marathon to raise money for charity. After Allen and I did our 20-mile training run three weeks before the marathon, I sent out my solicitation letters asking for people to donate whatever amount they wished per mile. I was living at Holy Name Cathedral in Chicago at the time, and a parishioner who lived in the John Hancock Building turned in his pledge form indicating a pledge of $100 per mile. Since a marathon is 26.2 miles, I thought perhaps he meant to make a total gift of $100, but his check was attached to the pledge form, made out in the amount of $2,620.00! That was precisely the motivation I needed, since I was determined not to have to return that check. Since that time, fundraising for charity has become a regular component of my marathon running. In 22 marathons over 22 years from 1995 to 2016, I have raised $462,363.16 for various charitable causes. That comes to an average of $21,016.51 per marathon, or $955.30 per mile. Not a bad rate of return for my efforts!

Another important component of my marathon running is prayer. Sometimes I do my marathon training runs with other marathon runners, but often I run alone. One of the ways I pass the time while running is through prayer. Some of the time I will say many Hail Marys on a small finger-rosary with 10 beads. Other times I pray for people by name so that my prayer becomes a sort of litany. In fact, in addition to seeking donations for charitable causes, I also invite people to send me prayer intentions that they would like me to include in my prayers while I'm running. I have received many moving requests from people asking for prayers for loved ones who are sick, unemployed, or recently deceased. They also request prayers of gratitude to God for favors received. Between fundraising for charity and praying for various intentions, my marathon running has itself become a sort of ministry that motivates me to keep going.

While I am still running and playing hockey, I have also started coaching since becoming bishop of Springfield in Illinois in 2010. I assist with the coaching (particularly of the goalies) at Sacred Heart-Griffin High School in Springfield. Not only has it been fun for me to get involved in the game of hockey from a different perspective, but interacting with the players, their parents, and the other coaches in the context of hockey has allowed me to get to know these members of my diocese and for them to get to know me in ways that would otherwise never have been possible in the usual avenues where parishioners meet their bishop.

Many of my best friends are people that I have been playing hockey with since college or with whom I have run marathons. I am sure I will also be friends for life with my fellow coaches and some of the players that I have been coaching. That is truly one of the real blessings of all sports.

Finally, when I lead the hockey team in prayer before games, I always start by praising and thanking God for the ability to play the great game of hockey. I ask the Lord for the grace to put some particular virtue into practice, such as discipline, dedication, or determination. I pray for God to help the players play to the best of their abilities, to keep them safe and strong and free from all injury and harm, and finally, for them to have fun! After all, as Pope Francis likes to remind us, the whole point of our faith is the joy of the Gospel! Jesus shows us the way to be happy both in this life and forever in the life to come. May God give us this grace. Amen.

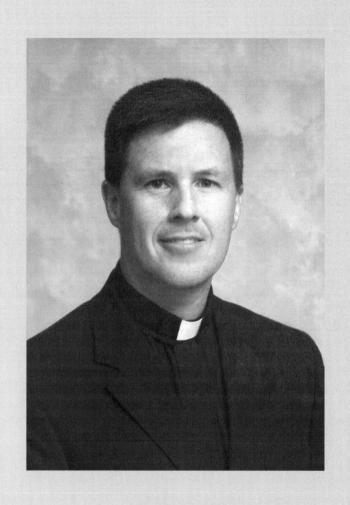

FATHER
KEVIN DREW

Run as to Win

IN THE 1986 MOVIE *HOOSIERS*, about a small-town basketball team that won the state championship, a frustrated teacher complained to the newly-arrived basketball coach that "Basketball players around here are treated like gods." With a tinge of sadness, the washed-up coach responded, "You know, most people would kill to be treated like a god, if just for a few moments."

I entered St. Peter's Catholic grade school in Quincy, Illinois, in 1972. The playground at recess was a massive sea of boys and girls playing all sorts of games. The boys' games invariably involved a ball of some sort — and if a boy did something heroic with the ball, then he would indeed be treated, if ever so fleetingly, like a god. At least until the bell rang and we lined up to say the Pledge of Allegiance.

My grandma once came to a junior high football game of mine. I remember her being mortified when it was over because my elbow was swollen and bleeding. It had taken a beating from all the tackles I made that day. For some strange reason, no one on the other team seemed to want to block me all day. It was a football player's dream come true.

I can understand my grandma's concern, but at the time, it was one of the best days of my life! People cheered as, over and over again, the man on the loudspeaker would say, "Tackle on the play by number 10, Kevin Drew." I am 50 years old, and I still have scars from that game; scars I would not trade.

There is ritual involved in sports, and there is hierarchy. There are coaches and captains and a special uniform to wear. There is the social reward that comes from belonging to a team. And there are few things more enjoyable, after being confined to a school desk for eight hours, than running all over a spacious and green ball field.

One particular rite of passage for me occurred in sixth grade at St. Peter's, the time when the boys started serving Mass. Serving was kind of like sports: Ritual and hierarchy were involved, and we wore a uniform — a black cassock and a white surplice.

The 1917 *Code of Canon Law*, the laws of the Church in force at the time, stated Catholics have a duty to foster priestly vocations. Serving at the altar did just that. It was a natural thing for an altar boy to consider the priesthood. When a young man found himself in a privileged position in the sanctuary, he automatically asked himself, "Could I see myself celebrating Mass? Would God call me to be a priest; a man of sacrifice?"

Some boys were more comfortable in the sanctuary than others, and I seemed to be one of the more comfortable ones. I appreciated the solemn ritual and the reverence: the genuflecting, bowing, lighting candles, ringing bells, and holding the paten under people's chin as they received Holy Communion.

In eighth grade, they gave me an award for "knowing the facts of the Catholic faith." This other kid, Jimmy Newman, got the award for actually *living* the Catholic faith. Ha! I figured Jimmy could be a priest, and I would get married and have lots of children like my father did.

There were, however, connections to priests in my family. My Grandma Schmidt, the one who came to my football game, kept house for a priest, Msgr. Casimir Toliusis, for 29 years. Two of her sons, my uncles Anthony and Carl Schmidt, are priests. They were ordained on the same day in 1950 for the Diocese of Springfield, Illinois. Growing up, though, I did not get to see these priests all that much, as they lived a few hours away. But I always admired them at reunions or funerals. They were a presence in their black clerical clothing, set apart from my other uncles and cousins. That made an impression on me.

Some impressions are so big that they are crucial dividing lines in one's life, events that leave a long-lasting mark. They are called "watershed" events. I had a watershed moment on Halloween afternoon when I was in seventh grade. The Quincy Notre Dame (QND) Raiders, my future high school, played their crosstown rival, the Quincy High Blue Devils, in the soccer regionals. The Raiders' record was 25-1, with their only loss coming from the Blue Devils earlier in the year.

The Raiders destroyed the Blue Devils that day, 5-1. Toward the end of the game, the QND star, Gary Koetters, dribbled the ball into the corner and then slipped it through the legs of a Blue Devil defender who will remain nameless. I will never forget the "agony of defeat" look on his face right after the ball went through his legs. It happened right in front of where I was sitting. Koetters glided around him and crossed the ball to Jim Thomas, who headed it in for his fourth goal of the game. As the crowd went wild, I said to myself: "I've got to do that. I've got to play soccer for QND."

In what was one of the first clearly defined goals of my life, I resolved to be the first freshman at QND to ever start on the varsity team. I didn't share that goal with anyone; I just started quietly pushing myself, practicing in the backyard and running — a lot. That would be my edge. You see, I was small. I was going to have to make up for my lack of size with grim determination and the ability to run my opponents into the ground.

"Run as to win!" St. Paul instructed the Corinthians. Saint Paul must have been an athlete at one time. And it would seem he had to be in pretty good shape to keep bouncing back from all the beatings he took. Somehow, I think St. Paul might have been looking after me when I was younger, although our goals were quite different. I was running for a crown of leaves that withers. He was running for a crown that was imperishable (see 1 Cor. 9:24).

On the first day of high school soccer practice, our coach made us run up and down a big hill in the park. At the end of that session, some kids were ready to throw up. I remember seeing at least one boy cry. It was excruciating, and my lungs burned like they never had before. But I survived. I had trained my body and disciplined myself in order to endure.

I did indeed become the first four-year starter at QND. I was a captain and an all-state player my junior and senior years. We made it to the state finals my sophomore and senior year, and then the next three years, when I was in college, my small high school of around 600 students finished second, first, and third in Illinois, beating large schools of over 3,000 students along the way.

In high school, I played with four players who went on to play professionally. I myself went on to play NCAA Division I soccer at Northern Illinois University, where I started my freshman, junior, and senior years. We played some of the best teams in the country, such as national champions Saint Louis University, Wisconsin, and Michigan State.

I actually played soccer very competitively almost every week until I was 32. Reflecting on it, I see that soccer was obviously a big part of my identity. We are, after all, what we do. And what could be more enjoyable, after being confined to a work desk for eight hours, than running all over a spacious green field?

My work life was nowhere near enjoyable. I had a modicum of success in the bottled water industry, but something always seemed to be off, even though I couldn't exactly put my finger on it. My goal was to find a nice wife and settle down in a nice career, but, slowly and painfully, it became clear that God was calling me for another kind of mission.

My father died when I was 32, the same year I quit playing soccer. Earlier that year, I had sat with him on his back porch. I remember asking him how he did it — how he had fed and clothed nine children and put all of them through Catholic school. He paused, took a sip of his drink, and quietly said, "I married your mother."

After my father's funeral, my priest-uncle Fr. Anthony took me aside and, without saying anything, took off his Roman collar and jacket and told me to put them on. And then he had someone take our picture. I remember thinking, "What is he up to?"

My mother was widowed at 61. When I would call home, our conversations would become more and more focused on the Catholic faith. Then guest subscriptions of Catholic magazines and newspapers, courtesy of my mother, started appearing in my mailbox — and I actually began reading them. When I went home, she would have priest vocation articles strategically placed throughout her house so I couldn't miss them. Ha! The poor woman was really working overtime.

One day, my mom called, said she was going to Israel, and asked me if I wanted to go. I said, "No," but she went anyway. The following year, she called again and told me she was going back to Israel — and that she had bought me a ticket. In the sales business, that is known as "assuming the close." The second time my mother did not ask me whether I wanted to go or not; she just assumed I would, and thus she closed the deal.

So, led by Fr. Mitch Pacwa of the Eternal Word Television Network (EWTN), we traveled all over the Holy Land. I walked where Christ had walked. I bent down to kiss the spot where He was born in Bethlehem, the spot where He died on Calvary, and the spot where He was laid in the tomb. On Good Friday, I traveled the crowded and narrow streets of Jerusalem as we prayed the Stations of the Cross. How many people can say they did things like these? How truly blessed I was — and am. And of course, it was all due to the gentle nudging of my mother.

Another watershed event in my life happened just off the crowded and narrow streets of Midtown Kansas City, Missouri, in 2001. I don't recall the exact day, but I do know it was a Tuesday in summertime. I was working in the area and on my way to get a slice of pizza at Joe's By the Slice, located in the back of Kelly's Westport Inn. The reason I knew it was Tuesday was because Joe had dollar slices on those days.

In any event, there are three very old inner-city churches within 30 yards of each other, just north of Joe's. It is not the best neighborhood, so I had always buzzed by this gauntlet of churches, and just always assumed they were not Catholic. But on this day, for whatever reason, I drove slowly, and something made me look at the sign on one of the churches. It said "Noon Mass." I had to do a double-take and looked more closely at the sign: "Our Lady of Good Counsel Catholic Church." I decided the pizza slice could wait and parked my car. I walked up the stone steps to the triple doors and noticed the cornerstone on the north side with "1906" on it.

Once inside and past the small vestibule, my eyes feasted on a small but immaculate church. Automatically I was drawn to the gorgeous marble high altar up in the sanctuary. And sitting on the altar was a beautiful golden monstrance that contained the exposed Blessed Sacrament. That helped explain the silent reverence all around me. Also on display in the sanctuary was a large image of the Risen Christ, with rays of light emanating from His Heart.

Along the back wall, a large number of people were standing in line. They were all going to Confession. I wondered, "Was it a holy day?" No. It was just lunchtime on a summer day in Kansas City. I couldn't recall the last time I had seen a line like that for Confession. I thought to myself, "What's going on here? What kind of world have I just stumbled upon; this heavenly oasis in the Midtown Kansas City desert?"

A priest who appeared to be pushing 80 exited the confessional and proceeded to say a very reverent and holy Mass. When Mass was over, he took out his rosary beads and knelt down. He started a prayer, during which he said, "Eternal Father, I offer you the Body, Blood, Soul and Divinity of Your dearly beloved Son, our Lord Jesus Christ, in atonement for our sins and those of the whole world."

My mother later informed me that the prayer was the Chaplet of Divine Mercy. She told me about Sr. Faustina Kowalska, the Polish nun who took dictation from Christ Himself in the 1930s and was charged with spreading His message of Divine Mercy.

The old priest's name was Msgr. William Blacet. At age 70, he was sent to Our Lady of Good Counsel Parish with the expectation that he would shut it down and retire. When he first got there, he had five or so people attending daily Mass, and he would collect around $100 at the weekend Masses.

As God would have it, word got around that there was a priest in Westport — one very dedicated to Our Lady and the Rosary, who heard Confessions every day over the lunch hour.

Good Counsel, a once broken-down parish slated to close, became a thriving parish with beautiful liturgies and splendid sacred music pouring down from the choir loft.

As I write this 15 years later, Msgr. Blacet is still there as the pastor. He is now 94, and one of his famous lines is, "I wasn't ordained to retire." Through the years, his fatherly example and fortitude has fostered many vocations to the priesthood. I can happily say that I am one of them.

I applied as a priest-candidate for the Kansas City-St Joseph Diocese, which was painful and a bit embarrassing because I was then already 40 years old. Of course, all throughout this time, I received gentle coaxing and encouragement from my mother. My younger brother Matt's encouragement came a little more bluntly. After I mentioned I was worried about what people might think, I remember him telling me, "Who cares what people think? God is the one calling you, not them."

Matt was right. There was a gentle voice that kept popping up in my head through the years. It was a voice I initially laughed off. After it kept coming back, I tried my best to ignore it. Then perhaps I even got a bit angry at its incessant bombardment. But it wouldn't go away, so I finally surrendered my will. I finally took the road that God had been calling me to travel ever since he formed me in my mother's womb.

With the fatherly assistance of Msgr. Blacet, I was accepted to study for the priesthood in the fall of 2006. That was the same year that the diocese announced that Our Lady of Good Counsel Church would be the diocesan shrine dedicated to Divine Mercy.

In January 2007, I started my first year of philosophy studies at Holy Apostles Seminary in Cromwell, Connecticut. Holy Apostles began as a seminary in 1957 in order to cater to older vocations, which at that time would have been men around the age of 25. When I attended, some of my fellow students there were men in their 60s. So at Holy Apostles (or, as some like to joke, "Holy Fossils"), I began the slow process of being formed into a new man — a man of prayer, study, and sacrifice.

Father Drew and Msgr Blacet in 2007 at the diocesan Shrine
of Divine Mercy, Our Lady of Good Counsel.

I received a degree in philosophy from Holy Apostles and, after my very blessed time there, I entered Kenrick-Glennon Seminary in St. Louis for four years of theological studies. Kenrick was more challenging in many ways because most of the men studying there were much younger.

At Kenrick, I felt a connection to St. John Vianney, the patron saint of priests. Vianney was on the way to priesthood when the anti-Catholic nightmare known as the French Revolution exploded. Afterwards, when the seminaries reopened in France, Vianney, then a young man, found himself taking classes with schoolboys. The boys assumed Vianney was some sort of dunce, but he was not; his vocation had simply been delayed.

We had a revolution in modern times that exploded in the late 1960s, known as the sexual or cultural revolution. It was an anti-Catholic nightmare that saw seminaries and convents empty overnight. I was in grade school and high school from 1972-1984, so I lived through the aftershocks. Upon reflection, I can see that my vocation, my calling from

God, was always there; just like Vianney's response to his vocation, it, too, had simply gotten delayed.

So, like Vianney, I endured the humiliation of taking classes with much younger men. Unlike Vianney, I probably really was the dunce of the class! I was always amazed at the intelligence of my younger classmates. And they were amazed how I, a man old enough to be a father to many of them, could run circles around them on the soccer field in the back of the seminary!

I, of course, took great pride in that. Too much pride. And I would pay for it later. After dominating my opponents on the field, I would have to sneak down to the ice machine for a bag of ice to nurse my wounds. Then at chapel early the next morning, the younger men would grin as they watched me limp over to my pew and gingerly genuflect to Jesus in the tabernacle.

So justice was done, and everyone was happy. Indeed, seminary life, though the workload was heavy and the pressure was on, was a happy time. I mentioned that I did not see my uncle priests too often growing up, but, after I entered seminary, I saw them more and more. What a blessing they have been, providing me with invaluable perspective, counsel, priestly fraternity, and wonderful laughs.

A man enters his fourth and last year of seminary after having been ordained a deacon. Two days before my diaconal ordination, against my mother's warning, I decided to play indoor soccer. I ran into the boards about 20 seconds into the game and split my lip. I don't know what hurt worse: the four stitches or the look on my mother's face when I got back from the ER. She cried, "You have to get your picture taken with the bishop!" Ha.

I got ordained, busted lip and all. The next year, I was ordained a priest. I offered my first Mass at Our Lady of Good Counsel with my two priest-uncles and Msgr. Blacet concelebrating.

I have been ordained for four years now, and though this has been a time full of blessings, it has not been without challenges and struggles. But what are these challenges except the cross our Lord commanded us to carry daily? So I carry the cross with joy, my clearly defined goal being to preach Christ Crucified and win souls for Heaven. Nothing else really matters to me. Like St. Paul writes: "For to me, to live is Christ; and to die is gain" (Phil 1:21).

How do I stay on this road God called me to travel? Much like I did for soccer. I cooperate by training my body and soul and being open to the graces He bestows on me. I listen to my mother — both of them; my biological mother and Our Lady, the Mother of Priests. Then every day, I go up and down a hill, but I no longer sprint. Instead I slowly go up to the altar of God. No longer is it my lungs that burn, but rather my heart as I gaze on the large crucifix in the church sanctuary.

The true High Priest hangs there, thirsting for souls, in the perfect and Eternal Sacrifice. Blood and water gush forth from His Heart as a fountain of mercy on our poor lost world, while I, acting *in persona Christi* (in the person of Christ) as priest-victim, thirst with Him.

So I'm running the race to win for the simple reason that I want to be treated like a son of God, but not for just a few fleeting moments. No — I'm racing for eternity. After I run the race, I want to show Christ the scars I collected in His service. Scars I acquired defending Him. Scars I would not trade for anything.

That, then, is my clearly-defined goal. My hope and prayer is that Christ answers, "Well done, good and faithful servant. You ran to win. Now, here is your imperishable crown."

Father Marsolle with family on the day of his first Mass in 2012

FATHER
KARL MARSOLLE, FSSP

Taming a Restless Heart

IS SPEAR FISHING OR FREEDIVING or any other sport the reason I became a priest? Of course not. But in retrospect, have these sports and activities given me a structure and a discipline in life that in turn helped me answer my call? There is no doubt. Do these sports and activities still help me engage in healthy recreation in order to better carry out my priestly duties? Most certainly. Operating from the principle that grace builds upon nature, the better ordered nature is, the more it can welcome and foster grace.

My name is Fr. Karl Marsolle, and I am a priest of the Priestly Fraternity of St. Peter (FSSP). I attended Our Lady of Guadalupe Seminary in Denton, Nebraska, for six years of intense formation and spent my seventh year as a deacon in Fontainebleau, France, ministering at our parish there. I was ordained to the priesthood on May 19, 2012, and am currently stationed at Our Lady of Fatima Chapel in Pequannock Township, New Jersey, after two years at St. Joseph's Parish in Richmond, Virginia.

I did not always live in such cold places. I was born in the tropics—in the French Caribbean, on the island of Guadeloupe. My family has been there for a while (since the 16th century on my dad's side). French is the main language there, and Creole, the local dialect. Being from an island where the ocean is always within a reasonable walking distance or a 15-minute car ride, sailing, boating, freediving, and fishing are pretty much in our blood. My grandpa was one of the pioneers of spear fishing in Guadeloupe. He won tournaments as far down the Caribbean as Curacao. He passed on his passion for the ocean to my dad, and my dad passed it on to his sons and daughters.

My dad was (and still is) quite the sportsman. In his youth, he competed in cycling and shooting. He was a clay shooting champion in Guadeloupe and Martinique, and went on to be selected for the French national team. My dad is also a freediver. Perhaps this is a good time to define our terms. Freediving is a form of diving that relies on the diver's ability to hold his breath until resurfacing rather than on the use of breathing apparatus, such as scuba gear. It is truly a serious (and dangerous) discipline made possible only through much learning and precise technique. It requires cardiovascular efficiency, the ability to depressurize as one gets deeper and deeper (lest one blows out his eardrums!), the ability to slow down one's heartbeat (to consume less oxygen), and so much more. My younger brother, who is in his late 20s, can hold his breath for more than three-and-a-half minutes while diving (even longer when he's just holding still underwater) and can dive down to depths of 120 feet. You add a speargun to the equation, and he comes back up with wondrous fish.

Of course, this is only possible after years and years of training. In my family, one first learns to swim, and then one learns to dive. I recall getting my first speargun by my sixth birthday. My dad would take me around the reefs in shallow water, and I quickly learned all the different types of fish and their behavior, the poisonous ones to keep away from, the sound of a spiny lobster under water, how to spot an octopus' lair, which sharks to beware of, what to do when the current is strong or when the water gets murky, etc. I would follow him to deeper waters, staying at the surface and looking 50-75 feet down through the crystal clear water as he dived and fished.

I was 8 the first time I saw sharks under water. Three reef sharks, about six feet long (they seemed enormous to me at the time!), came around my dad. I was frightened, but he kept his cool, continued fishing and, when he had completed his task, we calmly departed.

It has always been a great lesson to watch my dad in what he does — his composure, his attention to detail, his discipline. On his boat, everything has its place. There is a proper way to store gear, to reel lines, to tie fish hooks. There are rules and there is order. Order becomes especially vital when trolling (trailing a baited line behind the boat) or deep sea fishing, when we can no longer see land anywhere around us, and the boat becomes surrounded by schools of mahi mahi, ray-finned fish usually weighing 15 to 30 pounds each. Without the order my dad insisted upon, things would have become chaotic rather quickly.

Since I was a kid, my dad would take my brothers and I trolling. Sometimes we would go out trolling for two days and actually spend the night in the middle of the sea. A catch of anywhere around 600 pounds of fish would be considered a good trip. Occasionally we would even get lucky and reel in big yellowfin tunas (anywhere from 80 to 200 pounds) or blue marlins (300 pounds and above). A few months ago, my dad went out by himself and caught three blue marlins! At age 58, he still does some type of fishing at least twice a week.

In my early teens, the whole family moved to the United States very unexpectedly, because of a job opportunity for my dad. He would have been plenty satisfied staying in Guadeloupe, but he saw it as an opportunity for us. He worked very hard as a paper plant manager for eight years before returning permanently to Guadeloupe. We spent a year in Florida and then seven years in Nevada. It was a bit of a culture

shock for me, as I only spoke a few words of English. My two brothers and I were put in public school. It took a bit of adjusting, but within six months, we understood and began speaking English more easily, and soon enough we got the hang of things. The campuses, buildings, sports fields, and facilities in our new country were very impressive. Classrooms with carpeted floors and air-conditioning were quite a change from the open air classrooms I was accustomed to in Guadeloupe!

One of the aspects of the United States I found absolutely fantastic was that you could play sports for your school. In Guadeloupe's schools, there were no sports teams, and we had physical education class only once a week. Sports were extracurricular activities we did on our own, which my mom always took to heart. She had us start, among other things, water sports and tennis. The last thing she wanted for her kids was idleness. Now, living in the United States where sports and recreation were made so readily available, my brothers and I couldn't wait. I soon realized that I was too thin to compete at football and too short to compete at basketball. When my brothers and I discovered that wrestling was an option, we signed up right away.

Wrestling was great conditioning, offered great camaraderie, and was quite an experience to compete in. By his sophomore year, my older brother was Zones Champion of Las Vegas. When we lived in Nevada, Utah and its phenomenal ski slopes were only about a three-hour drive away, which made it easy for my dad, my brothers, and I to take up snowboarding. This new sport reminded me of surfing in some ways, and, with time, I became more competent and grew in confidence.

However, just when I thought things were coming along so well, I underwent a large setback: A jump did not quite work out the way I had planned. When I woke up the next day, I could hardly move and learned that I had spent the night in the hospital. I had suffered a major concussion and could have broken my neck. This was definitely a setback for my sporting plans. I had to give up wrestling and most sports for a time, had migraines more often (I had experienced them a little bit before), and newfound neck pain. Never in my life had I been in such a weak state. I had no endurance for any activity, and I couldn't make an effort without sharp headache pains. My vision was also affected so that reading and studying were strenuous and difficult. During this time, my prayer life became more regular. Since I could not depend on my own strengths and abilities at all, the only logical option was a deeper search for the Lord so that He would heal me and so that He would be my strength.

Only after eight months of intense pain did I start seeing small improvements. As soon as that happened, I started conditioning at a gym for the purpose of getting back into sports. At that time, I also took up golf, not because I had any inclination toward the sport, but because I wanted to compete with my older brother who had taken a liking to it. Las Vegas then had about 36 golf courses, and the junior program was affordable and very well organized. As the conditioning and working out at the gym progressed, I took golf lessons and started devoting lots of time to practice. The high school I attended had one of the best golf teams in Nevada, and I was able to make the team my junior and senior year. I reached a level of competence where playing for a college team became a possibility.

Since I also felt I had recovered well from the snow-boarding incident, it seemed like the right time to combine weight training with an intense cardio component. I joined a boxing gym, which was an intensity increase compared to the previous gym I had been training at. The summer following high school graduation, I tried out for the golf team at Allan Hancock College, a junior college in Santa Maria, California, and made it. My plan was to play there one year and transfer to a Division I team the following year. The Lord, however, had different plans. Within the first semester of college, it became very clear God was calling me to serve Him.

All the expectations I had for college were lining up and happening. Yet I couldn't help but feel a certain emptiness, a disappointment. I often thought to myself: "Ok, after this, then what? Is this it?" I wanted more from life, and all the things I thought would make me feel accomplished left me dissatisfied. At the same time, two of my college roommates were Protestant. They realized I was Catholic (thanks to a picture of Our Lady of Guadalupe in my room), so some heated discussions started.

To my great shame, I did not know the Bible or even the Gospels; indeed, I realized I did not know my faith well at all. Yes, I went to Mass on Sundays, and I said my prayers every night, but I couldn't explain or defend the little that I knew. It is hard to describe, but I felt like I could not let this occasion pass by. There was definitely grace at work like I had never felt before. I started looking into apologetics (explanations of why we believe what we do) and lessons of pure and simple Catholicism.

I started reading the actual Gospels for the first time in my life! It was then that I received the grace of my call: The words of our Lord calling the apostles to follow Him struck deep into my heart. I had never had an experience quite like this. It was as if these words were addressed to me directly. As I kept on reading St. John's Gospel, I came to the eighth chapter and this verse from our Savior: "And you shall know the truth, and the truth shall make you free" (Jn 8:32). I felt like I had been struck by lightning, that my life was about to change forever, that my world had been turned upside down ... and yet there was such a sense of deep peace and joy.

It became clear in an instant that I was being shown the doorway to my purpose and meaning in life. I wanted the freedom of which Jesus spoke — the freedom which only He can give. God had called. I could do nothing other than answer. About two weeks later came the end of the semester. I left college and everything I had worked toward thus far. I started my search to answer God's call. Through the advice and counsel of excellent priests I met, I entered a Benedictine monastery a year later in Southern France, called Sainte Madeleine du Barroux Abbey. I wanted to explore a possible monastic vocation. Little did I know that by this time, my brother had already pawned my custom-fitted golf clubs. Apparently he knew something about my future.

I spent a year and a half discerning with the Benedictines in France. The rhythm of life at the Abbey was very different from anything I had ever experienced. *Matins* were prayed every morning at 3:30 a.m., followed by *lectio divina*, Holy Mass, specific times for mental prayer twice a day, classes, and manual labor. *Ora et labora* is the Latin version of the Benedictine motto "Pray and work." For the first time in my life, there was not much room for sports. Only minutes of volleyball a day (in silence, mind you!), an afternoon hike for all novices once a week, and a *grande promenade* every three months where we would attend Mass directly after *Matins* and take off all day for a grand hike in the beautiful countryside of Provence. We would come back late at night, singing *Compline* (evening prayer) by memory under the stars. If I thought there was order on my dad's boat, the monastery had it on an even grander scale. The rule and structure of life were a wonder to me: 60 monks, coming from all sorts of different backgrounds, nationalities, and mentalities, united together for the beautiful ancient Latin liturgy, all centered on the Lord.

After a year and a half at the abbey, I had already received the black monastic habit of St. Benedict and a new name when my superiors and I discerned that my call was not to monastic life, but seemed to be to the priesthood. With a heavy heart, I left the monastery, thankful to our Lord for the incredible experience and journey. My novice master had strongly recommended I apply to the FSSP and wrote the necessary recommendation letter. It seemed God's will was clear enough: He was calling me to the beautiful, ancient (yet timeless) "extraordinary form" of the liturgy and the support of community life, which are our Fraternity's charism. He advised me to try to join the North American District instead of the French District, since I had lived in the U.S. for several years. He did mention I would probably enjoy recreation and sports more there, and he was right.

I will always treasure the time I spent at Our Lady of Guadalupe Seminary in Nebraska. The days were full and quite busy with common prayer, classes, studies, exams, duties, chant and other liturgical practices, spiritual conferences, ordination preparations, and, yes, *sports*. It seems seven years is a short time to learn everything a priest must know. Thankfully, the formation never stops during the life of the priest, but I am convinced the Lord makes full use of those seven years to prepare the candidates as much as possible.

In my time at seminary, it seemed so obvious how our Lord's words to St. Peter were fulfilled when Peter asked Him in Matthew 19:27: "Behold we have left all things, and have followed thee: what therefore shall we have?" The answer: a hundredfold and life everlasting. I have always considered the brotherhood and camaraderie I found at seminary to be part of that hundredfold the Lord speaks of. He is never outdone in generosity. How many dozens of brother priests the Lord has blessed me with! It has become clear, with the approval of my superiors, that I was being called to the Fraternity's traditional liturgy in the context of community life.

In seminary life, one is supposed to pray hard, study hard, and *play* hard. I will always remember seminary for the beautiful liturgy, the beautiful chant (especially at Christmas and Holy Week), some of the fantastic philosophical and theological courses, and, of course, the sports field. We had extremely talented athletes playing a variety of sports from all over the globe: the U.S., New Zealand, Mexico, Scotland, England, Australia, Croatia, and Canada. There were weeks where we would have the occasion to play sports five to six times a week. There was much to choose from: basketball, rugby, volleyball, tennis, soccer, football, ping pong, etc. We often had tournaments in different sports, with different sections challenging other sections, such as philosophers vs. theologians, first year students vs. fourth year students, and so forth.

We had tournaments against other schools and seminaries a few times a year. When the weather got too harsh, the weight room and punching bags would be in use. The facilities since then have gotten even better. Thanks to the generosity of donors, a gymnasium was built with a full basketball court, running circuit, a weight and cross-training area, and an area where we could play indoor soccer. The gym is in use nearly every day. This is because recreation is an art; it promotes a good balance. There is nothing like a good 90-minute soccer game after finals week. There is nothing like a good game of rugby or football to help one then pray better and sleep better. Of course, anything in life can be taken to excess, but seminary time showed me the necessity of recreation, of balance, of blowing off steam in order to handle situations well, in order to serve God better. And that's the whole point. Everything is ordered towards God and striving to better accomplish His holy will.

Now in the parish, the level of sports is, of course, not as competitive, but I have kept up with athletics for leisure and good recreation. In every parish I have been at, there has always been a group of young guys who are interested in playing team sports on a weekly basis. In some parishes, it is soccer; in others, dodgeball or flag football. I haven't been in a parish yet where there was an interest in freediving or spearfishing, but maybe one day! I haven't given up on golf, either. Although I can never dedicate as much time to it as I used to, I still enjoy nine holes here and there a few times a year. Some parishes have a Knights of Columbus tournament and, if I am paired up with former college players, then it will likely be a winning experience. Otherwise, I will still enjoy a day outside and settle for the long drive contest.

Sports are not the reason I ended up at the altar. However, they have always held an important place in my life. In answering God's call to the priesthood, sports have been a great blessing because of the order and discipline they instilled — an order and discipline very similar to that needed in the spiritual life. I have always loved St. Paul's comparison of the spiritual combat to the athlete's training and performance:

> Know you not that they that run in the race, all run indeed, but one receiveth the prize? So run that

you may obtain. And every one that striveth for the mastery, refraineth himself from all things: and they indeed that they may receive a corruptible crown; but we an incorruptible one. I therefore so run, not as at an uncertainty: I so fight, not as one beating the air: But I chastise my body, and bring it into subjection: lest perhaps, when I have preached to others, I myself should become a castaway (1 Cor 9:24-27).

Although I could not see it at the time, in retrospect, the sports I devoted myself to were a training ground for natural virtues such as fortitude and perseverance. These virtues I unknowingly applied in answering God's call, engaging in the exercises of the spiritual life, one of which is the practice of prayer. Sports were a blessing God gave me and then ordered in my life towards Him, that I may serve Him better and ultimately love Him more. Unto Him be glory forever and ever. Amen!

FATHER
CHASE HILGENBRINCK

*From Soccer Nets
to Fishing Nets*

"DON'T YOU MISS SOCCER?"

I have been asked this question many times since announcing in 2008 that I would leave professional soccer and become a Catholic priest. From the wincing facial expression and heightened vocal inflection, I have perceived that those asking the question really mean something like, "Don't you think you have made a dumb decision?" I take no offense, and often let out a joyful laugh before answering.

Of course I miss playing the game at the highest level; I miss the camaraderie of the locker-room; I miss the travel; I miss running out of the tunnel into the stadium; and I miss living what was my dream — just to name a few things. But if the inquirer seeks to find out if I regret my decision, the answer is a resounding "NO" — and, given the chance, I wouldn't go back to playing the game, either. Not because I didn't love it, but because I found something better. In fact, something better found me when Jesus revealed to me that He had a plan for my life, and that nothing less would satisfy my heart's desire for greatness. As I look back at the trajectory of my life in hindsight, I can see clearly how the Lord used sports as the instrument that would help me see who I was truly made to be — *a fisher of men.*

I grew up a cradle Catholic in Bloomington, Illinois, with my brother, Blaise, and our parents, Mike and Kim. Since I now know the distinction, I like to describe my family when I was growing up as faithful, but not "on fire" for our faith. We attended Mass every Sunday without exception, went to Confession a few times per year, and said our daily prayers. Nevertheless, I speak for myself — and maybe my brother — when I say that our faith was not the most important aspect of our lives. Sports were the most important thing for us, and Mass seemed to get in the way.

When Blaise was 10 and I was 9, we were invited to play on a travel soccer team, the Hardees Stars. I remember the family discussion that took place before we decided to make this financial and time-consuming investment. Our parents told us that there were two requirements. The first was that the family would not be divided. This meant that we would not play on different teams and travel to different tournaments each weekend, but rather, I would have to play up a year on my brother's team. This endeavor would be a family-building opportunity. The second requirement was that we would never miss Mass — and we didn't.

Blaise and I believed in and loved God, but we didn't appreciate the fact that we were the family that was always taking a different path. For instance, if we knew that we had to play on Sunday mornings, instead of going out to dinner with the team, we would go to Saturday evening Vigil Mass. Or, if we played late into Saturday afternoon, we would go to Mass early Sunday morning, at times arriving late to our Sunday morning game. If we played late Saturday evening as well as early Sunday morning, we would get back to Bloomington in time to make the 9 p.m. Illinois State University Newman Center Mass. Looking back, I am impressed that my parents made all of this happen without Internet or GPS! For nine years, we would travel all over the Midwest with soccer games nearly every weekend, and no matter where we went, we found a Mass. At the time, I couldn't foresee the impact that my parents' example would have when I would later make

decisions about what sort of man I would become.

Blaise and I excelled on each of the teams for which we played all the way through high school. This made us realize that playing Division I soccer was a real possibility. While at University High School in Normal, Illinois, I was named to the All-American Team and privileged to represent our country after being selected to the United States Under-17 National Team. These honors caught the attention of many top NCAA programs. God guided me toward attending and playing for Clemson University in the Atlantic Coast Conference. Through our abilities in soccer, Blaise and I received scholarships — his from Southwest Missouri State University and later from Butler University — helping our parents pay for our college education. This was the first time that I saw sports as an instrument rather than a destiny.

Like any other maturing teen, I was well aware of and excited about the independence that college would bring. I was unaware, however, that I would face the most important decision of my life — that is, whether I would decide to be a practicing Catholic Christian. The practice of my faith suddenly became an option rather than an obligation. Without my parents telling me that I had to go to Mass and waking me up on Sunday mornings, I had the choice of whether I would go to Mass or not.

Like most people, I inherited the Catholic faith, but never made an intentional decision to be Catholic. However, I was never one to do something half-way, and, faced with the decision either to continue going to Mass once per week or dumping everything that my parents taught me, I decided that I would continue to attend. Moreover, I realized that no one else in college was going, which brought about a feeling of independence and making my own choices. To my surprise, I started to enjoy Mass for the first time. Because I had chosen to be there, I started to listen more closely to the readings and homilies; I actually prayed the prayers that I had previously only recited by rote; and I developed a passion to know what I professed to believe. I even started praying with my teammates in pregame huddles. In short, I made the faith my own, I decided to be Catholic, and while I wasn't yet living out that faith as a disciple of Christ in my daily life, the invitation to discipleship would soon follow.

While attending St. Andrew Church in Clemson, I was invited year after year to go on a student retreat. Although I was beginning to enjoy practicing my faith, I didn't feel like

I fit in with the "holy rollers" who hung out at the parish. I made an excuse every year about why I couldn't go on retreat. Nevertheless, in my senior year, when the soccer season was over — and I could no longer use that as an excuse — I finally went on the spring retreat. One of the spiritual exercises was a group *lectio divina*, or "divine reading," where we listened and meditated as the priest read a Scripture passage, waiting for the Holy Spirit to make a word or verse speak directly to us. I remember Fr. Bill reading chapter four of St. Matthew's Gospel. The words that stood out to me, after hearing them for the first time, were "fishers of men." When it came time for me to share the words that grabbed my attention, it was explained that this was the narrative in which Jesus called His first priests — His apostles — from their jobs as fishermen to their vocations as fishers of human hearts. While I thought Jesus was clever for His wordplay, I didn't connect the dots, didn't think that those words were speaking to me for any other purpose — even when one of the girls on the retreat told me before leaving that she thought that I "would be a great priest."

After winning the ACC championship in 2001 and making four NCAA tournament appearances — including two trips to the Elite Eight — I had the opportunity to pursue my ultimate dream, which was to play soccer professionally. In July of 2004, just two months after graduation, I went to play on a trial basis with Chilean First Division team Huachipato, and eventually signed my first professional contract. When my dream to be a professional athlete became a reality, I thought God was confirming my dreams as His will. While that was true, I now know that it was a temporary means to distinguish my profession from the priestly vocation to which He was calling me.

When I first arrived in Chile, I realized that everything in my life had changed. I went from a known to an unknown culture; from speaking English to speaking broken Spanish; from a fast-paced and exciting college life to a slow and "depressed" culture; from a social life filled with roommates, friends, and family to a place with no roommates, friends, or family. Moreover, I arrived in the middle of the Chilean winter, which meant about three consecutive months of rain.

In the midst of culture shock and loneliness, I learned two important lessons. The first is that human nature has the self-protective tendency to fall back on what one knows. The second is that there were only two things in my life that didn't change. Since they were the only two things I still "knew," they were the things that I turned to in my need. Those two objectively unchangeable aspects of my life were soccer and the Catholic Church. No matter where you go in the world, the rules of soccer don't change, and one can get along on the field even without knowing the language. The same is true of the Church. No matter where we go, despite a different local language, the Mass doesn't change, and Jesus is present in the tabernacle, waiting for us. He was certainly waiting for me.

I began stopping by *La Asunción* (The Assumption) parish, just a block away from my house, for nearly daily visits. For the first time, as I spent time with Jesus — not for pious reasons, but merely because I needed His comfort — I discovered what it was to have a personal relationship with Jesus Christ. That began an initial relationship of discipleship, which led to friendship, and eventually to consciously-perceived sonship. I remember one of those early days in Chile, sitting in that cold chapel, hearing the rain outside, praying for comfort, and inexplicably hearing the gentle booming of an inaudible voice inside of my heart say, "Be my priest." I wanted to believe that this "voice" was a product of my own thoughts; however, I quickly reasoned that I was not thinking about priesthood at the time, I didn't have any desire to be a priest, and it certainly wasn't my idea of comfort.

The idea of priesthood was not attractive to me at all. My idea of greatness as a man was the example that I had seen in other athletes, as reinforced by pop culture. I believed greatness in manhood equated to having a beautiful woman on your arm, having a lot of money, owning a big house, driving a big car, being popular, and going to great parties. Priesthood didn't offer any of those things. It offered no woman on the arm, no owning a house, owning only a simple car, not being popular, and no wild parties. Not only was the priesthood unattractive, but it also felt unmanly. Needless to say, my understanding of manhood and greatness needed to be recalibrated.

I also had some good excuses why I couldn't be a priest. For instance, I had a desire to be married and have children, to give my parents grandchildren, and to pass on the family name. I wasn't sure how I would ever be happy as a priest. I wondered if it was a lonely life. I felt unworthy — who was I to forgive sins or to celebrate the Eucharist?! On the heels of the notorious priestly scandals, I was scared to be identified with a vocation that many perceived as synonymous with perversion. Perhaps more than all of these things, I didn't want to give up soccer. I had trained my whole life to get to this point. I was living the dream of every kid — and man — in the world. I remembered saying to the Lord, "You have confirmed Your will over and over that I should succeed in this sport; why would You take it away from me now?" I would find out that my success in the game was for another purpose — that I would have a relevant story to tell, and that my soccer talents would not be taken away, but simply repurposed. Since I wasn't yet convinced by the Lord's first call, He began to speak through the game of soccer.

I spent the next two-and-a-half years trying to forget that voice and that call to the priesthood. However, it was on my mind every day and grew progressively stronger. Despite actively avoiding God's call, I thought I had found the comfort I was seeking. I had a great girlfriend, was a regular starter on my team, signed a new contract, had become fluent in Spanish, made many friends, experienced a small taste of fame, and was playing soccer in front of thousands of fans each weekend. The culmination of this experience came in the 2006 season, when I had been named the best player in the league at my position for the second consecutive year, and my team, Ñublense, won the league title. This is what I had dreamed about all of my life. The week after sealing our promotion from second to first division, parades and parties abounded. I remember at the end of that week sitting in my bed, unable to sleep due to the endless excitement, consciously acknowledging that this was the height of my happiness in life. At the very same moment, I realized two things. One: There was something still missing in my heart. I was happy, but not satisfied. Two: I had no other plans for my life. At the age of 25, I had experienced my dream; other than signing a better contract or playing in another league, I had no higher goals to set for my life. This was a shocking and decisive moment in which I was given the grace to realize that soccer would never satisfy my soul, nor would any of my goals or dreams satisfy the longing of my heart. More than feeling helpless, I humbled myself to realize that God had a dream for my life, and only His plan would satisfy my longing.

In December of 2007, after playing another year with Ñublense in the First Division, I returned to the States from Chile where I had been playing professional soccer for almost four years. I was ready to be back home, and although no one knew it at the time, the underlying reason for my return was because I had finally found the courage to begin the process of applying for seminary. Nevertheless, I was not yet ready to give up soccer. Since the Major League Soccer (MLS) season began in February and the seminary's academic year began in August, I wanted to finish my career by playing for six months in the U.S. in front of friends and family, who rarely caught my games in Chile.

There was a handful of Major League Soccer teams interested in signing me, but after praying about it, the Colorado Rapids offer seemed like the best fit. Not only was the coach interested in me becoming an immediate starter at the left fullback position (defender), but I also had several cousins living in the Denver area. The outlook in Colorado was great, so I headed to Denver knowing it was where God intended me to be. The only thing still weighing on my mind was that I had started the application process to become a seminarian for the Diocese of Peoria, but I had not yet been accepted.

After spending the preseason with the Rapids in Miami playing exhibitions against various other MLS teams, we flew back to Denver just a day before we were set to depart for London, where we would finish our preseason training with the English Premier League giant, Arsenal F.C. Before training that day, I had just gotten dressed at my locker when I was called into the head coach's office. When I saw him and the general manager sitting in the office with apologetic looks on their faces, I knew that something was wrong. The GM proceeded to tell me that, just weeks before opening day, the team still lacked a much-needed goal scorer, and in order to stay under the salary cap, they were going to waive my contract and release me from the team. I was in disbelief. I had only been "cut" from one other team in my life, and that was the Under-17 U.S. National Team, after spending a year with them and just before they went on to finish fourth at the World Championships in New Zealand. Moreover, judging by how smoothly the deal had gone from the start, I thought Denver was where God wanted me to be. On top of that, I had not yet been accepted as a seminarian, so the future seemed very uncertain.

That afternoon, in my disappointment, I didn't want to speak to anyone, and I couldn't think for myself, so I turned back to what I knew and decided to find a tabernacle. I needed Him, the One who had been guiding me all along to the priesthood, to make sense of this for me. Although I had been attending Mass at Denver's cathedral, I looked off the seventh story balcony of my cousin's apartment where I had been staying in downtown Denver, and I saw the steeple of a Catholic church within a few blocks. I walked to the church, but when I approached, the doors were locked. I saw another steeple a few more blocks away, so I continued walking. Providentially, it was open. As I entered the vestibule, I realized that there was a prominent Hispanic population at the parish, as I saw Spanish literature before entering the nave. As I opened the double doors to enter the nave, my eyes were immediately drawn to a banner that hung above the pews, stretching the entire width of this humble chapel. In Spanish, the banner read, "*Ahora serás pescador de hombres.*" Had I not spent four years in Chile, I would not have known what it said. But because I did, I not only knew what it said, but I unmistakably knew that the Lord was speaking directly to me. The English translation of the banner was, "Now, I will make you a fisher of men." Needless to say, I didn't take another step, but simply hit my knees right there in the back of St Joseph's Church and apologized for my lack of trust in His providence. There couldn't have been a clearer sign for me to understand that all of this was happening as a part of His perfect will. I knew that the Lord had not forgotten about me and that He had everything under control.

After remaining for a short time in awe-inspired prayer — as well as bittersweet thanksgiving — in the chapel, I decided to call my parents to tell them about being waived from the Rapids, as well as the providential "sign" of reassurance that I received. My parents were sympathetic, knowing my disappointment about the way the contract deal had gone down, but when the conversation moved to trust in God's will, they remembered that they had just received a letter in the mail from the Diocese of Peoria. Presuming that it was just another part of the multi-month seminarian application process, I asked them to open it in order to see what I needed to do next. To my surprise, it was a formal letter from Bishop Daniel Jenky, officially accepting me as a seminarian of the Peoria Diocese! The Lord couldn't have spoken any more clearly, nor given more assurance to my heart of His guidance, His providence, and His intimate care for my vocation. I immediately packed my things and began my 14-hour trip back to Bloomington, Illinois, with plenty on my mind to pray about.

After spending two weeks at home, I was invited by Fr. Brian Brownsey, my new vocation director, to meet up with my future seminarian brothers at Peoria's cathedral for Holy Thursday. That night at Mass, I was given the grace to identify the fact that I was still lamenting the way my soccer career had ended, which had left a bad taste in my mouth ... even if it was God's will. I felt torn up inside — happy that God's will for me to enter seminary was confirmed, but disappointed that my will was not done — that I would not share the last months of my playing career with my family and friends. On that Holy Thursday, I remember kneeling in the cathedral, gazing upon the crucified Christ, and finding the strength to completely resign my will to God. I mustered the words, "If playing soccer these final months is not what You want for me, then I don't want it, either. I am not going to continue to play this game of self-pity."

I truly trusted that God's plan was superior to my own. Those who know Jesus know that He has a sense of humor. The very next day, Good Friday, I got a call from my agent, Shep Messing. Although we had not been in touch since I left Denver, he told me that I needed to be in Boston on Easter Sunday to start playing for the New England Revolution. Initially, I told him, "No." Not only had I just told the Lord that I understood that His will was that I not play anymore, but it was also Easter Sunday. When I got off the phone and spoke to my parents, my dad calmly shared some very simple, yet sage advice. He said, "Chase, sometimes God closes doors because He doesn't want you to walk through them, yet He opens others so that you will." We quickly decided that I would go to Boston on Sunday and that I would train for a few days, continuing to discern the Lord's will, before signing the contract.

In those first few days, my primary discernment was whether or not I would tell the Revolution of my plans to leave in just a few months, now knowing for certain that I would enter seminary in August. I knew that God's will for me was to be transparent, and again, I was given the grace to identify that this inner debate was caused by my fear that this door would also close. I needed to deny my own will and place my future with the Revolution — or without them — into the hands of God. His will was revealed again, in a most providential way. The night before I was set to speak to Mike Burns, the GM, to reveal my plans to leave the team in July, my agent, Shep, called me. He had just received a call and a contract proposal from Mike. Shep proceeded to tell me that there was a unique detail that they wanted to discuss with me. He said that while Burns and Coach Steve Nicol had received very good scouting reports about my abilities on the field and had seen me play live for a few days in training with the team, the signing was a bit rushed because Opening Day was just a week away. Therefore, Mike said that they wanted to offer me a short-term contract with an extension clause that would come into play on July 1. I couldn't believe what I had just heard. I think that Burns feared that I would be the one to close the door on the contract; nevertheless, the contract would end in July, exactly one month before I had to enter seminary! This door was left open in a providential way, and I walked through it.

I played my final semester of professional soccer with the Revolution, and in July of 2008, when I was offered an extension to my contract, I declined and announced my retirement. Just a month later, I entered Mount St. Mary's Seminary in Emmitsburg, Maryland, as a seminarian. In 2014, I was ordained a priest of Jesus Christ in the Diocese of Peoria, Illinois, and I am more satisfied in my heart today than I have ever been in my life. More than happiness, God has graced me with more peace than I have ever known. I will be forever grateful that He allowed me to experience the beauty of sports, opened my eyes to the greatness of manhood, and blessed me with the privilege of being called to be a *fisher of men.*

Father Wells (center) with other members of the DC Padres

FATHER
DAVID WELLS

*Discovering Wells of
Strength in Divine Mercy*

PAINTED WITH VERY BROAD STROKES, my childhood memories are divided between the Catholic faith and sports. In very different ways, these two entities contributed to my personality: the faith forming me spiritually, while sports contributed to my human formation. As the sixth of eight children, I looked up to my older brothers and sisters. I was blessed to find in them witnesses of living the faith, and, in my brothers especially, passionate aficionados of, and competitive participants in, sports.

Although my relationship with God as expressed through my Catholic faith and my love for sports were distinct realities in my life, I found that they went hand-in-hand in some way. To begin with, both my faith and sports involved ritual and repetition. Daily prayer was part and parcel of growing up in our household, as I remember things such as Mom praying with me before bed and the whole family praying the Rosary during car rides. Similarly, playing catch or a game of one-on-one basketball were my favorite daily activities with my brothers. Going to Mass on Sundays was a ritual that consisted of putting on my Sunday best, blessing myself with holy water upon entering the church, kneeling down to pray and prepare for Mass, singing, receiving Holy Communion, and, if we were lucky, stopping by Dunkin' Donuts on the way home.

In sports, there was the routine of putting on my soccer uniform on game day, warming up before the game, eating orange slices at half time, and, more often than not, celebrating a victory after expending myself physically for 60 minutes. Both the faith and sports had their distinctive vocabularies and expressions that could only be understood and shared with those who participated with you in those spheres. Whether it was "Peace be with you" at Mass or "Whaddya say, kid?" on the baseball diamond, both were signs of intimacy and shared participation. As I looked up to my older brothers and cousins as good athletes, I similarly looked up to my Uncle Tommy as a priest.

I knew that both faith and athletics require a willingness to sacrifice and endure a degree of suffering in order to excel.

When I was 2 years old, my brother Kevin (a teenager at the time) swung a bat without noticing that I was right behind him. It hit me square in the eye. I was wailing in pain, and at one point, my mom said, "David, what can I do to get you to stop crying?" Through heavy sobs I was able to explain why I was really inconsolable: "I want to go back outside." On other occasions, there would be bad bounces from ground balls that squared up with my mouth, but whatever the injury suffered, this was all part of the experience of playing the game. There was an analogous reality in the realm of faith. The suffering of fasting, the angst of confessing, the struggle of straining to remain quiet in prayer for 20 minutes: These were all essential and accepted aspects of living out the faith. I knew intuitively that to participate fully, whether in my faith or on the ballfield, accepting suffering was somehow at the heart of it.

As I entered high school, both my faith and my athletic ability would be tested in ways that would entail a deeper level of suffering. I attended DeMatha Catholic High School (in Hyattsville, Maryland, a suburb of Washington, D.C.), known nationally for its storied athletic programs. When I was cut from the freshman basketball team, it was my first experience of not making a team — not an earth-shattering event, but a new and challenging one, nonetheless. During summer breaks beginning after my sophomore year, I would work for my father's masonry construction company. D.C. summers are

notoriously hot and humid, so this work was not for the faint of heart. After long days of hauling buckets of mortar, bricks, and cinderblock up and down scaffolding, I'd be "beat-tired." Some days I would arrive home, shower, go right to bed, and not wake up until it was time to get ready for work again. On other days, I had American Legion baseball games in the evening, so I would drive straight from work in the awful D.C. traffic to games an hour or two away. My teammates nicknamed me "Powder," as I would arrive at the games still caked in the mortar I was dealing with all day. One positive thing about working construction is that it certainly got me a lot stronger — and I needed all the strength I could get to bolster my scrawny 5'6" frame!

On one of those summer work days, about a week after finishing my junior year of high school, my life changed forever. My oldest brother, Danny, then vice president of the company, arrived on the job site where my older brother Mike and I were working. He pulled Mike and me aside to speak to us privately. "You'll remember this day for the rest of your life," he started in a serious tone. "Uncle Tommy was killed last night."

My Uncle Tommy, a priest of the Archdiocese of Washington, D.C., was a holy, fun-loving man. He was always ready to crack a joke or, in some cases, to crack your head with one of his famous knuckle-protruding "noogies." He took the faith utterly seriously, and the rest of life — including himself — he took lightheartedly. He was the source of my first real impression of the priesthood, and I was struck by just how human and relatable he was, while also upholding the dignity of his priestly identity. He drew his life, energy, and love from his relationship with Jesus Christ in the Eucharist. He was the linchpin of our family, hosting Thanksgiving and Christmas dinners for our large family. He celebrated family Baptisms, First Holy Communions, and marriages, while silently stepping in to aid in family crises.

When the news of his tragic death broke, I had no idea how to respond. There are no words to describe the shock and sorrow I experienced upon hearing that a homeless man who frequented the area around my uncle's parish had murdered him in a botched robbery. I remember asking God, "Why would You permit something so senselessly evil?" It was as if my uncle were snatched away from us during the best years of his priesthood. All the memories that we would have continued sharing were stolen away. Although I couldn't see or imagine it at the time, much good would come from my uncle's death, including my own first hint of a call from God.

It was at Uncle Tommy's funeral Mass that for the first time I was struck by how powerful the priesthood is when it is lived well. Far from being a lonely life, it allows you to connect with and positively affect numerous people. I met so many people that loved Uncle Tommy and were profoundly changed by his ministry. It was evident how much he loved them, as well. Even today, 16 years after his death, I frequently meet new people that were profoundly influenced by his priesthood. I was attracted to this life, which seemed adventurous, joyful, and fulfilling. At 16 years old, having just finished my junior year of high school, the seed of a vocation was planted within me. I wrote a letter to my dad, and in that letter, almost in passing, I mentioned that I had wondered if God might be calling me to the priesthood.

Yet there was so much else going on in my life — I was just beginning to date, and I had high hopes for my senior year baseball season. The thought of the priesthood was pushed to the backburner. My junior year baseball season was a success, all things considered. The team didn't win the conference championship, but I managed to work my way into the starting lineup and, by the end of the season, I was batting leadoff. As I entered my senior year, I had lofty individual and team expectations, and yet that season would be one of the most humbling experiences of my life.

Although I could always hit well, my fielding became an issue. I suddenly couldn't throw the ball accurately from third to first. Once something like that gets in your head, it's certainly hard to overcome. I ended up sitting out halfway through my senior year because my fielding was a liability. The third base starter just happened to be my next door neighbor, and a freshman at that! Ughh! That was a tough one to swallow. It was tough picking him up and driving him to and from the games, knowing that he was starting over me. Of course, he was so humble that I couldn't get angry at him. God sometimes has a loud and clear way of communicating to us, and He clearly communicated to me that baseball was not in my future.

I entered the University of Maryland in the fall of 2001. My freshman year began in a surreal way. The terrorist attacks of 9/11 occurred about two weeks after having moved onto campus. Two weeks after that, a huge tornado ripped through the school, taking the lives of two young girls and severely damaging much of the campus. In the midst of a traumatic first month, I found what would be one of my greatest supports in the Catholic Student Center at the University. The campus chaplain, Fr. Bill Byrne, reminded me so much of my uncle. He was fun-loving and faith-filled, which made the priesthood look like an attractive vocation. Father Byrne was persistent in asking me to discern the priesthood. I attended many of the Center's vocation events, as well as the retreats they offered each semester.

I was being tugged in two directions, though. A young man I had played baseball with in high school was the president of a fraternity, and he insisted that I look into joining. I decided to join the fraternity, so part of me was attracted to the spiritual opportunities offered at the Catholic Student Center, while another part of me wanted to live it up in a way that I wasn't proud of in my heart of hearts. What saved me during this first time living away from home without supervision was my desire to attend daily Mass and weekly Confession. The grace of God would slowly prevail in me, inspiring me to leave behind old habits and temptations, and to give my life more fully to Christ.

Our family had a unique vacation every summer. While other families might go to the beach or mountains, we went to the horse races. On a Friday at the beginning of every August, we would wake up at 5 a.m., pack the family station wagon, and drive seven hours north to Saratoga Race Track in New York. If everything went well, we would be there in time to make the first race at 1 p.m. sharp. During that week dedicated to the horses, we stayed at a resort in Western Massachusetts and would drive an hour and a half to and from the track every day. On Tuesdays, the track was closed, though, and we had to find another way to spend the day. As God would have it, the town next to our lodgings was Stockbridge, where the National Shrine of The Divine Mercy is located. On Tuesdays, then, we would participate in Mass, Confession, and the Chaplet of Divine Mercy at the Shrine (an excellent form of reparation for the money spent on losing horses). During our yearly vacations, I became more acquainted with the Shrine, its history, and its purpose, and I became enamored with its patron, St. Faustina.

After my sophomore year in college, we took our usual family vacation to Saratoga at the beginning of August. On Tuesday, since there was no horseracing, I headed over to the Shrine at 3 p.m. for Confession and the Divine Mercy Chaplet. I remember as I entered the confessional that it was hot and stuffy. I peered through the screen separating confessor and penitent, and I was able to discern by the zucchetto he wore that my confessor that day was a bishop. After confessing my sins, he asked me whether I had ever thought about the priesthood. Hot, sweating, and wanting to avoid the question at that moment, I replied in the negative. He gently encouraged me to pray about it, and asked me to reflect on Proverbs 3:5-6:

> Have confidence in the Lord with all thy heart,
> And lean not upon thy own prudence.
> In all thy ways think on him,
> And he will direct thy steps.

These verses impacted me, and I did begin to pray about the possibility of a vocation. The idea of a vocation to the priesthood — the seed of which had been planted in me after my uncle's death — began to move off the backburner.

A year later, as I was preparing to enter my senior year of college, my future weighed heavily on my mind. I was an international business major with a minor in Spanish, and two job possibilities appeared for me. I could continue to work in my father's construction company — but not as a laborer! — or apply to teach high school Spanish at DeMatha High School, where I had first fallen in love with the language. That summer, we headed up to Saratoga for our yearly vacation. On Tuesday, with no horse races occurring, I went to the Shrine of The Divine Mercy for Confession before the 3 p.m. Chaplet. I remember that, just like the year before, it was hot and humid. As I entered the confessional, I peered through the screen, and was surprised to see the same zucchetto I had seen the year before. After confessing my sins, I heard almost exactly the same response I had heard the year before: "Good confession; now tell me, have you ever considered the priesthood?" This time, I was prepared, and I responded very differently than the year before. "Yes! I have thought about it. In fact, you asked me the same question last year when I was here, and you told me to meditate on Proverbs 3:5-6." Our interaction in the confessional that afternoon seemed providential. It was as if God were speaking to me through the bishop hearing my confession.

As I returned for my senior year at the University of Maryland, I decided that I should get a spiritual director to help me discern my calling. Since I was minoring in Spanish, I decided to knock on the door of a nearby parish, where I knew there was a priest from Colombia who was once stationed with my Uncle Tommy. Father Dorsonville — now Bishop Dorsonville — gladly accepted my request. In our first meeting, he inquired about my thoughts on a vocation to the priesthood. I told him that I was unsure, and his response disconcerted me somewhat: "You'll know soon." Father Dorsonville really encouraged me to pray about it seriously. I did so, and on December 8, 2004, I told him in wavering Spanish that I thought God was calling me to the priesthood. (I didn't plan on the Solemnity of the Immaculate Conception being the day

I would decide to enter, but Our Lady under that title would continue to guide me throughout my time in the seminary.)

I applied to Mount St. Mary's Seminary in Emmitsburg, Maryland, for the Archdiocese of Washington, D.C., and was accepted in the spring of 2005. One of the great blessings during my five years at Mount St. Mary's Seminary was the ability to continue playing sports. The seminarians would organize intramural teams to compete with college students in the University's intramural leagues. It was a blast to play against the college kids in football, soccer, basketball, softball, and even dodgeball — and win our fair share of games along the way! I was the seminarian chaplain for the University's men's lacrosse team for four of the years I was at the Mount. It was a great opportunity — and a challenge — to try to keep these young men focused on their spiritual lives as a top priority. As I remembered so well, it is terribly easy to go astray spiritually while in college.

While I was in the seminary, a priest I know began a seminarian and priest basketball team called the DC 'Hood (with '*Hood* being short for *Priesthood*). They would play against local parishes that organized their own teams and invited the kids of each parish to come out and watch the games. One of our players would give a halftime talk promoting vocations to the priesthood. It is so important for younger kids to see priests as real human beings who love the same things that they love, including sports. This opens up the possibility for them that God might be calling them, too.

I was ordained to the priesthood on June 19, 2010, at the National Shrine of the Immaculate Conception, in Washington, D.C. — 27 years to the day after my Baptism! After ordination, a brother priest mentioned to me that he was planning on forming a seminarian and priest baseball team, modeled after our DC 'Hood basketball team. "There's no way that would work," I thought. Basketball is one thing, but baseball is a tougher one to pull off, logistically. Undeterred by my doubts, he formed the DC Padres baseball team, which is now in its sixth season of play. We compete against local Catholic high schools and invite families to come out and enjoy the experience. If you would have told me, upon finishing my baseball "career" after my senior year of high school, that in 10 years' time I would be a priest *and* playing baseball again, I would have had a good laugh.

It is amazing that, as the Catholic faith and sports were so influential in my childhood formation, so now as a spiritual father, I help to form a younger generation through those same means. Whether it is teaching in the classroom or celebrating the Sacraments, playing basketball at recess or baseball with the DC Padres, all of it is done to foster in younger kids a real relationship with God.

I find sports to be a great bridge, a great way of reaching those who may be under the impression that to be religious, prayerful, and/or a priest requires you to be something other than human. One of the surprises for me in the priesthood is that the Lord does not remove your natural gifts and talents upon ordination; on the contrary, He continues to use them, except now for a new purpose: that in all things, He may be glorified.

FATHER
JOSEPH FREEDY

Heaven Begins on Earth

"All that we call human history [is] the long terrible story of man trying to find something other than God which will make him happy"

— C.S. Lewis in *Mere Christianity.*

THAT'S MY STORY; THAT, IN SOME SENSE, is your story. Here's the question: What's your "something other than God?" The most popular ones are money, power, pleasure, or fame. A lot of the smaller ones involve control: trying to control our Church, our government, our families. We think that if we can force every aspect of our lives to fall into place, then we will be happy.

For me growing up, my "something other than God" was the praise of other people. I grew up as the youngest of five children in Bethel Park, Pennsylvania. We were raised in a solid Catholic home, and were very familiar and friendly with some incredible priests. We would often invite them over for dinner, which normalized them to me. I was fascinated by them and thought they had very exciting, adventurous lives. Hearing them talk to my family about their experiences as priests was amazing. They led pilgrimages all over the world. They went on mission trips. When they preached, they spoke incredibly about God's love for us. Unconsciously, I looked up to them as one would to an uncle. I thought that I'd like to be like them one day, so the seed of a vocation to the priesthood was planted in my heart early on.

Like so many Catholics, though, I lacked a true understanding of my faith. I went to Mass regularly, but I was never very engaged; it was just what we did as a Catholic family. I spent most of my days as a kid playing football with friends in our backyard. Football is a huge deal in Western Pennsylvania, and since my two older brothers played, I wanted to play as well. My older brother, David, was a great athlete and an inspiration to me. But when I was 13 years old, he died of stomach cancer while studying medicine at Vanderbilt University. It was a traumatic experience for all of us.

For a guy just beginning his teenage years, which are tough enough, this tragedy seemed unbearable. David was the hero of my life. He was smart, good-looking, and extremely good at sports. He had an outgoing, dynamic personality, so it was just very natural for me to look up to him. When he died, it was the first time that I had ever started to ask deeper questions about the meaning of life, about suffering, and about the afterlife. It was a young age for me to be asking those questions, but when you are confronted with tragedy, those questions come to the forefront. For the first time in my life, I believe the Lord was stirring up a lot of thoughts about vocations and life's purpose.

While those thoughts and questions never left me fully, at the time, I tried to bury them. I threw myself into football. I began to build my entire identity around football and used it to fill the interior void in my life. Despite having a wonderful, loving family, I grew up with a lot of insecurities, which began in grade school and continued even into college. I started to use football as a way to be accepted, to try to be the person that I thought everyone wanted me to be.

As a result, religion was set aside while I focused on football and on being accepted by everyone. I turned into a star player at my high school in Bethel Park, but in truth, I could have given more, pushed myself more. I was a good player, but not a hard worker. I simply practiced and loved to compete. While I was skilled enough to earn a scholarship to play football at the University of Buffalo, I received a wakeup call when I found myself riding the bench behind three other quarterbacks during my freshman year.

Like so many college kids, I wandered. If I couldn't be a great football player, then I could become popular by being a partier. I still went to Mass on Sunday and was "religious" in a sense, but anxiety filled me, and my sense of self-worth stemmed from my popularity and athletic skill. I turned to the party scene to try to fill the void within me, as so many college students do.

That time in my life was enlightening for me. I certainly wasn't actively discerning at the beginning of college, but I was searching nonetheless. While God didn't want me to experience that typical college culture, He brings good out of all things. But the path that strays from Him doesn't lead to happiness. So often today, we hear: "Throw off all the rules. Don't let anyone tell you what to do. Freedom!" That's not wisdom. That just leads to chaos. The freedom that God desires for us is a freedom from fear and a freedom for authentic love. We were created to make our lives gifts of loving service. Our happiness comes in using our freedom to love and serve others. We are made in the image and likeness of a God who gives Himself away in generous love, and so while the world tells us it's all about us, to turn inward in a selfish way and to hoard, the only way to authentic happiness is to give ourselves away in love.

At this point, I was following the worldly understanding of freedom, and so something in my life had to change. One of the first things that changed me was meeting and beginning to date a special girl. Her authenticity attracted me. She didn't try to be what everyone wanted or expected her to be, like I tried to do at that time; she was simply herself. She helped to pull me out of some of the garbage I had sunken into, and this was such a gift.

Football, surprisingly, also helped me turn around. After a series of injuries to the several guys who were ahead of me, I assumed the starting position for the 1999 season and took on the responsibility of leading the football team. I was the starting quarterback for three years in Buffalo, where people also take football very seriously. My role as the team leader helped me to become less self-involved and more convicted about my life.

That seed that was planted so early in my childhood remained and pulled me towards the priesthood, however slowly. My life changed forever one Christmas when I had come home from college. My dad always read the Bible and another spiritual book before leaving for work in the morning, and he happened to have *The Lamb's Supper* by Scott Hahn on his end table during the time I was home. The book really opened my eyes because it related so much to my own life. The first chapter perfectly described my Catholic faith: The Mass was such a familiar thing to me, yet I didn't know what it was beyond the surface of the memorized prayers.

This book helped me to begin to look past the outward appearance of the Mass, and what I found began to draw me in. I started to learn about and, for the first time, understand the Mass and appreciate it for what it is. I came to understand that the Eucharist is not just a sign or a symbol, but that it really is the Body, Body, Soul, and Divinity of Jesus, and that everything in the Mass has profound meaning. All the gestures and all the symbols are an expression of God's love for us and our desire for love. The Eucharist is where these two desires meet most fully. That was the first time that I really began to understand that the Mass is a foretaste of Heaven, that it is Heaven on earth. The big turning point was when I began to meet God through this. He ceased to be a distant idea or a nice philosophy and became real. I realized that He is a personal God, and that His love makes a difference.

Peace, joy, and love began to fill my heart, very much akin to St. Augustine's experience. He, too, looked everywhere for happiness and fulfillment, but only realized after years of searching that it was God, Who had been right in front of Augustine all along, that he was looking for. My heart's deepest longings would be satisfied in the Mass like I had never thought possible. Our thirst for God is met by God's thirst for us most profoundly in the Eucharist.

When I went back to school at the end of Christmas break, I was determined to go deeper into my faith and share what I had learned with others. I went to a group called the "Fellowship of Christian Athletes," but found that many of the ideas presented there opposed what I was taught as a Catholic. So I went before the Lord in the Blessed Sacrament and asked Him what to do. I spent a lot of time with Him, asking Him to reveal His plan for me. During the time I spent in quiet prayer with the Lord, I sensed that the Lord might be inviting me to the priesthood. While I was so much happier than I had ever been before, I was also very reluctant to let go of my own designs for life and pursue this calling. By that point, I had been in a serious relationship with my girlfriend for a few years. Though I was happy with her and ending the relationship was a difficult decision, I realized that the Lord had a different plan for me. God's plan is the best plan for our lives and is what will make us most happy.

They call the Lord the "hound of Heaven" for a reason. He kept putting on my heart this subtle invitation to the priesthood. It kept growing inside me until I was able to take a few steps of discernment and say, "Yes, this is what God is calling me to do." Eventually, I met with a vocations director, who encouraged me to surrender to God's plan for my life.

In 2002, I graduated from the University of Buffalo with a communications degree. I then entered Saint Paul Seminary in Pittsburgh, Pennsylvania, and began studying philosophy at Duquesne University. I was subsequently assigned to the North American College in Rome, where I earned a master's degree in marriage and family studies while at the Pontifical John Paul II Institute. During this time, I saw how much Rome is saturated with grace; there is so much history there, so many saints, and so many visible testaments to the Christian faith. I'm so grateful to have spent time there, as it was a great faith-building experience.

While in Rome, I had the opportunity to meet St. John Paul II and be an altar server for Pope Benedict XVI. I began studying in Rome in 2005, the year that St. John Paul II died. The first time I met St. John Paul II, I had prepared something to say, but when he came up to me, I just opened my mouth and started crying. The love that radiated through him was overwhelming. I wasn't expecting that. He patted me on the face, gave me a big smile and a hug and said, "God bless you."

The death of St. John Paul II was very sad, but it was very beautiful at the same time. His massive funeral attracted attention from all over the world. I saw the family of God come together during that time in Rome, which was a powerful experience for me. I will reflect and meditate on the strong faith of God's people that I witnessed there for the rest of my life. We then welcomed our new Holy Father, Pope Benedict XVI. What a blessing both men have been to the Church!

On June 21, 2008, I was ordained a priest at St. Paul Cathedral in Pittsburgh, Pennsylvania. In the days before I was ordained, I knew I was born to be a priest. Upon my ordination, I knew in the most profound way that this was who God made me to be.

I have been serving as the Vocations Director for the Diocese of Pittsburgh for the past seven years. It has been an incredible joy, but there are challenges to building a culture of vocations. Perhaps the biggest challenge is convincing young people that God is alive and real and has a perfect plan for our lives. He has prepared a vocation for each and every one of us from all eternity. Jeremiah 1:5 expresses this concept: Before God formed us in the womb, he knew us. Our lives are not accidents, but perfectly prepared and provided for by God. I want others to know the contentment that I experience as a priest, and I do that by helping them to realize their own calls.

The life of the priest is a deep life. We don't live on the surface; it's not about money, pleasure, or power. The life of the priest is about living a sacrificial life, bringing Christ, the only one that we really need, to the people. It's a life worth living.

The most amazing thing about the priesthood is acting *in persona Christi* — "in the person of Christ." This is what occurs in Confession: The priest says not "Jesus absolves you," but rather, "*I* absolve you." It also occurs in the Mass: The priest says not "This is Jesus' body," but rather, "This is *my* body." We are the mediators between God and humanity, which is such a beautiful and profound thing: God has called *me* to do this. It's so wonderful that it is difficult not to cry when thinking about it. Sometimes I have cried even while acting *in persona Christi* because I'm struck by the love God has for His people. The humility that God shows by allowing mere men to act in the person of the Only Begotten Son is an amazing thing. To know that my hands have been anointed to bring the Body and Blood of Christ to the world and to forgive sins is such an indescribable blessing. The gift of the priesthood overwhelms me. I've been ordained for over eight years now and have never experienced an unhappy day as a priest.

Men spend their lives running from God's will for them, when that will is precisely what will make them most happy. Jesus invites people to follow Him so many times in the Gospels. Answering "yes" to that invitation is a profound step towards an indescribable adventure. Pope Benedict XVI visited the young people gathered at World Youth Day in Cologne, Germany, in 2015 and told them, "The happiness you are seeking, the happiness you have a right to enjoy has a name and a face: it is Jesus of Nazareth, hidden in the Eucharist." Relationship with Jesus through His Body and Bride, the Church, is the communion that we all long for. No matter what, nothing can separate me from His love (see Rom 8:38-39), so my happiness is not dependent on my circumstances or how I feel in a particular moment. It's a deep joy and a realization that my Heaven has begun on earth.

BISHOP
JOHN BARRES

From College Point Guard to
Point Guard for the Church

This chapter is dedicated to all my coaches and teammates through the years who have inspired, pushed, and challenged me. It is also dedicated to the spiritual directors, brother priests and bishops, and the People of God who have coached me in the ways of "holiness and mission."

THE HOLY SPIRIT MOVES at every moment in every one of our lives. The Holy Spirit has moved in my life in a call to the priesthood and a call to be a bishop.

My parents, Oliver and Marjorie Barres, were Protestant minister converts who met each other at the Yale Divinity School. They entered the Catholic Church in 1955, and my father wrote a book entitled *One Shepherd, One Flock*, recounting the story of my parents' decision to become Roman Catholics.

They were attracted to the splendor of truth in the Catholic Church and the doctrine of apostolic succession — our belief that we can trace the lineage of Catholic bishops through the centuries directly back to the apostles, and ultimately to Christ Himself.

In God's Providence, one of the consequences of my parents' courageous decision to put truth first in their lives was that on July 30, 2009 — 54 years after their conversion — their fifth child of six was ordained a Catholic bishop, thereby becoming part of that line of apostolic succession that led them to Catholicism.

Every priest and bishop has a unique story to share about how he discovered and responded to his vocation. In addition to the narrative of my parents' conversion and courageous decision-making, which so dramatically affected where God would lead them and their family, I also have had athletic experiences in which the Holy Spirit formed and shaped me, and which have been deeply connected to my call as a priest and bishop.

Early Basketball Experiences and
St. Augustine's Parish CYO Basketball

My large family moved into a new house in 1964, and I can remember going into the backyard and discovering a basketball court. I picked up a basketball for the first time at the age of four and could not make my "shots" reach the basket, but have been hooked on the game ever since.

I can remember being determined to play Catholic Youth Organization (CYO) basketball as a fifth grader (the only one on the team) on the fifth-sixth grade team at St. Augustine's Parish in Larchmont, New York. It was a memorable gym with spin-dial scoreboards and a bicycle horn used as a buzzer.

From seventh to eighth grade, we were coached by Joe Gallick, a 6'5" Iona College player from the early '70s who both looked like and admired New York Knick Phil Jackson — a somewhat marginal player with a huge heart and non-stop hustle and drive. Joe sensed something great in the character and spirit of Phil Jackson, and Jackson's subsequent brilliant coaching career confirmed Joe's intuition.

Joe was my basketball mentor. He really taught all of his players a love for basketball, the fundamentals, and the history of the game. The team was fast, quick, and clever, so he taught us the press of renowned UCLA coach John Wooden.

Joe patiently melded together some very spirited personalities with different kinds of games. He took us to the Nassau Coliseum to see "the Doctor" (Julius Erving) play for the Nets. Joe drove a beat-up Camaro convertible with holes in the roof. We caught his love for the game and the importance of real commitment to improvement.

To that end, he encouraged our team in the summer of 1973 — between seventh and eighth grade — to go to the John V. Mara CYO Sports Camp, sponsored by the Archdiocese of New York and run by the basketball coach and players of Cardinal Hayes High School.

It was, in the best sense, a basketball boot camp — constant drills and running, some personal time with a Holy

Cross College assistant coach who helped me hone the Jerry West-style jump shot I was aspiring to, and many games from morning to night. I think all of us came away from those two weeks with an even deeper commitment to hard work. I never improved as much in a two-week period as I did then.

One of my most vivid memories was of Terence Cardinal Cooke (now a Servant of God) flying in on a helicopter and landing on the baseball field. I remember making a point of going over to him to shake his hand, and I remember the peace and goodness in that gentle, holy face.

I was also a good gymnastic tumbler and vaulter during this period. I always felt that my experience of round-offs, handsprings, and flips on the gymnastic floor helped me develop aggressive drives to the basket, an emerging jump shot, and all the in-the-air transactions that are part of basketball. I ended up choosing basketball over gymnastics in eighth grade, but have always been grateful for the top-flight gymnastics training I received at Hommocks Middle School.

With my parents' encouragement and sacrifices, my four sisters, my brother, and I pursued athletics in a united, mutually encouraging, and supportive way. My brother was an outstanding baseball player and a precocious student of the effective baseball swing. We grew up on Bayard Street, and so the Bayard Street neighborhood sports experience was also critical to my development. The neighborhood was filled with boys of all ages, so with creativity, initiative, and negotiation, we organized daily touch football and tackle football games, Wiffle ball, stick ball, Wiffle ball golf, and hours upon hours of basketball. We all have great memories of these games, the brotherhood we shared, and the communal sense of relating boy to boy, and family to family.

Larchmont Little League

Some of my most powerful and emotional childhood memories revolve around the Larchmont Little League. These occurred at the time of the Apollo moon launches in the spring of 1969.

I was 8 years old and was being drafted onto a new expansion team in the Larchmont Cap League called the "Space Cadets."

At the time, "Space Cadet" had no derogatory connotation, but after our winless expansion season, we might very well have been responsible for creating it. I made contact with the baseball just once the entire season. Like most young Little Leaguers, I experienced moments equivalent to the Wide World of Sports' "Agony of Defeat," but also moments of Little League Glory.

After my first seasons as a Space Cadet and a Maroon Monster, I had a great two-year run of championships that began with playing first base for the Corner Store Pirates and winning the Minor League championship. I remember making a lot of clutch hits and some gymnastics-aided diving catches, but I also remember committing an error late in a game near the end of the season that prevented us from being undefeated. This experience led me to dive into the backseat of the family car crying, but I also had the resilience to make a comeback after that game-losing error and have a sparkling championship series.

Then in my first year of the Majors on the Village Ford Cubs, we had an unbelievable experience of team chemistry and momentum. We were a mediocre 6-4 in the regular season and then ignited in the playoffs, beating the Mamaroneck Fire Department Foxes in the championship.

In the late innings of the final championship series game, I made a series of clutch plays at shortstop. I robbed one batter of a single up the middle with a horizontal diving catch on a grounder. Sprawled on the ground, I touched second base for the out, jumped up, and threw a runner out at home plate for a unique double-play that helped prevent the Foxes from mounting the late inning rallies they were known and feared for.

The following year, I seemed to lose the magic touch I had had for fielding at shortstop, and I made some embarrassing errors in the field. In one of the early games, with my newly-drafted little brother Bill playing beside me at second base, a pop-fly was hit clearly to the second baseman. As shortstop, I called Bill off the pop ... and dropped it — one of those stories between brothers that lives on decades later. We had a mediocre season that final year, but the Larchmont Little League experience resulted in my growth as an athlete, a person, a leader, and an invested young member of the Larchmont community.

Caddie at Winged Foot Golf Club

I found out about caddying at Winged Foot Golf Club through my next door neighbor and my best friend's father, who was a friend of the caddie master who assigned caddies to golfers and managed the tee times of the golfers.

Winged Foot hosted the U.S. Open in 1929 (won by Bobby Jones), 1959 (Billy Casper), 1974 (Hale Irwin), 1984 (Fuzzy Zoeller), and 2006 (Geoff Ogilvy), as well as the 1997 PGA (Davis Love III). It will host the 2020 U.S. Open. At the 1974 U.S. Open, I had a chance to immerse myself in golf history when, as an eighth-grader with a caddie badge pass, I watched every round of what became known as "the Massacre at Winged Foot," chronicled by sportswriter Dick Schaap, when former University of Colorado football player Hale Irwin won the U.S. Open at 7 over par.

I normally do not associate the U.S. Open with the Mass and the Eucharist, but Dick Schaap tells a story about Bobby Jones at the 1929 U.S. Open that involved the Mass: "After Bobby Jones' twelve-foot putt forced the 1929 Open into a playoff, USGA officials notified Jones and co-leader Al Espinosa that their thirty-six-hole playoff would start at nine A.M., the next day, a Sunday. Jones, always the gentleman, suggested that the starting time be pushed back until ten so that Espinosa, a Catholic could attend Mass. Sunday morning, at St. Vito's Church near Winged Foot, Al Espinosa was at Mass; so was Bobby Jones, who was not a Catholic."

What an extraordinary story of what it means to be a Christian gentleman. Bobby Jones not only arranged for the tee time to change so that Al Espinosa and his wife could attend Sunday Mass but, as a non-Catholic, he attended the Mass himself with his Catholic wife Clara.

The story does not end there. On December 15, 1971, three days before his death, Bobby Jones converted to Catholicism and received the Sacraments on his death bed.

I like to think that Bobby Jones' generous and magnanimous Eucharistic gesture at the 1929 U.S. Open at Winged Foot helped prepare him to open his soul to the fullness of the truths of Catholicism and the grace of receiving our Lord in the Eucharist three days before he died.

I first went out to caddie in the spring of 1972 between sixth and seventh grade. We had heard that you had to wait on the caddie bench for a couple of days before the caddie master let you have a bag. This was a test of your commitment and whether you would stick with caddying.

That experience as a fidgety middle school boy sitting there with the other aspiring caddies, knowing that we had to master our natures in order to wait and be patient, eventually became an image of waiting and being patient in prayer. There is something about working through restlessness and waiting patiently in a caddie yard that would later become a symbol for me of working through restlessness and distraction in periods of silent prayer before the Blessed Sacrament.

Children can be quite intuitive about adults. This makes caddying a real education about human nature for a young person. Being with a golfer for four plus hours, sharing his experience of the ups and downs, glories and tragedies in a round of golf, allows you to pick up on character strengths and weaknesses. You pick up emotional shifts (good and bad) and mood changes. You react and work through them.

I learned about the sensitivity adults need to have in trying to encourage young people. I had some great experiences with golfers and I had a few very bad ones. But it was the bad experiences that most taught me as a priest and bishop to be as sensitive, patient, and supportive as possible with young people.

So often, just when we think young people are not paying attention, they get it completely. If we model the Gospel consistently, powerful seeds of faith can be planted at the most unexpected moments. In turn, children and young people of all ages, so often extraordinarily perceptive about adults, have a great capacity to evangelize and inspire adults with the freshness and vitality of their faith.

Yale Football Family History and the Influence and Encouragement of Yale Basketball Captain Mike Baskauskas

My uncle, Herster Barres, Yale Class of 1932, was the right end for the great 5'7" Yale quarterback Albie Booth, known as "Little Boy Blue." Booth was such a Yale legend that he actually has a verse devoted to him in the old-time classic song "You Gotta Be a Football Hero."

In just about any history of Yale football, you will find that Herster Barres' opening kickoff touchdown saving tackle and his 30-yard pass reception from Booth were critical factors in Yale defeating Harvard 3-0 in their 1931 game at Harvard Stadium. I have a picture in my office of my uncle in his Yale football uniform and had the privilege of personally donating on behalf of our extended family old reels of Yale football film, taken by my grandfather at the Yale Bowl during the 1929-1931 seasons, to the great Coach Carmen Cozza for the Yale football archives.

My father, Oliver (Yale Class of 1943), was much younger than my uncle. He used to join his father and the packed crowds of 70,000 at the Yale Bowl to see his older brother play. Yale football was a generational tradition, so my father took me at the age of 8 to the November 2, 1968 Yale-Dartmouth game to see legendary quarterback Brian Dowling and running back Calvin Hill. I was mesmerized by the atmosphere and pageantry — and by the exciting play of these two legends.

Just a few weeks later, Yale and Harvard, both undefeated teams, met at Harvard Stadium for a showdown, 37 years after the heroics of Albie Booth and Herster Barres in the 1931 game. Yale had a commanding lead and their fans were already waving their white handkerchiefs when Harvard scored two touchdowns and two two-point conversions in the last 42 seconds, resulting in a 29-29 tie. I cried over that game, and it made me realize that in the world of sports, as in life, nothing is totally predictable, that momentum can shift in a moment.

This Yale football context and tradition in our family led me, as basketball emerged as the sport I would focus on, to go to some Yale basketball games. Mike Baskauskas was the 6'4" Yale basketball captain from 1972-1974, and I saw him play against a great Penn team in March 1973. Yale was trounced in that game, but Baskauskas' hard work, relentless all-out hustle, and dedication made a lasting impression on me. I wrote a letter to him, and we began a correspondence in which he emphasized hard work, discipline, and dedication as the path to improving my game.

He sent me a large packet of ball-handling drill ideas and wrote: "Dear John, I believe you'll be a fine player someday. But you've got to realize that to be successful, you must totally commit yourself to your goal. If you want to be a super player, you should want to put in a super effort to work hard."

I eventually wrote a tribute piece to Mike Baskauskas in the Sunday *New York Times* Sports section when I was playing as a junior point guard on the Princeton junior varsity basketball team. Though I have never had the chance to meet Mike, his letters and support stoked my desire to play Ivy League basketball and have served as a constant point of reference for how to encourage and mentor young people effectively.

Andover Basketball and the Inspiration of St. John Neumann

I transferred to Phillips Academy (Andover) for my junior year of high school, starting in the fall of 1976. My father and uncle had attended the school, so there was a family tradition going. Fortunately, Andover gave me an excellent financial aid package that enabled me to attend.

The intensity and quality of the academics was extraordinary, and the competition on the varsity basketball team was just as intense. The team included the future Harvard 1981 basketball captain and a future Princeton football All-American safety. I can remember thinking at the end of varsity tryouts that I would most likely be cut, but as I went to the dining hall, I joyfully discovered that I was on the list pinned to the announcement board. I had made the team.

This team went on a tear with the talent we had playing for us, and somehow I ended up getting a fair amount of playing time as a fast and driven 5'11", 135-pound point guard, coming off the bench and playing intense pressure defense. It was a great experience, and my Andover teammates, like my Princeton teammates, are lifelong friends.

In January-February 1977, in the middle of this great basketball season, I wrote a paper on St. John Neumann, who would be canonized just a few months later in Rome by Blessed Pope Paul VI. The paper ended up being published in a few Catholic magazines.

Saint John Neumann's life of priestly missionary zeal, complete love for the Word of God and the cosmic power of the Catholic Mass, along with his humility and care for the poor, were a great inspiration to me. His life and priestly dedication hit me at an unexpectedly deep level.

Then one day at Mass, in the midst of writing this term paper on St. John Neumann and right in the middle of our winning basketball season, the priest raised the chalice at the consecration, and in silent peace, I asked: "Lord, do You want me to be a priest?" It was the beginning of my discernment of a call to the priesthood through the intercession of this great American priest-saint.

Saint John Neumann had been bishop of Philadelphia in the 19th century (he died in 1860), and the Philadelphia Diocese at the time contained the five counties that would much later (in 1961) become the Diocese of Allentown. As a junior in high school who was deeply inspired and moved by St. John Neumann's holy life, I never dreamed that I would be named his successor for the Diocese of Allentown, as I was in 2009. The Holy Spirit was deeply at work in my life in a rich way, just as the Holy Spirit is at work in all of our lives.

As the bishop of the Diocese of Allentown, I make periodic trips to the St. John Neumann Shrine in Philadelphia, asking the saint to intercede for me, to help me be a deeply holy and missionary bishop, and that the people of God of the Diocese of Allentown would be deeply holy and missionary. As I kneel before his body encased in the altar of sacrifice, I ask St. John Neumann to intercede for a rich harvest of holy vocations to the priesthood, just as he interceded for me to become a priest and his successor as bishop of the Diocese of Allentown.

Athletic Crisis and Conversion on the Andover Varsity Basketball Team

Many of our great Andover players had graduated by my senior year, so I had hoped to become the starting point guard. But I kept throwing the ball away in one preseason practice, and the coach demoted me to the second team.

I thought a lot over Christmas break and found a short pamphlet about dedicating your athletic life to Jesus Christ and the glory of God. It was a Christocentric, evangelical pamphlet, which I adapted to the fuller Catholic perspective on the objective truths of the Creed, the Sacraments, Catholic moral teaching, and prayer. I think the deeply-felt pain of losing my starting position made me open to considering this perspective.

My whole approach changed. I had always been deeply Catholic, but I had never connected my Catholic faith to my love for basketball. Though I might have appeared humble and modest to most people, I realized that I had been playing basketball in an ego-driven, rather than Christ-driven, way. That is why I was so crushed the day I lost my starting position.

When I returned from Christmas break, my attitude had changed; I was consciously connecting basketball to my very personal faith and prayer, and to the power of the Eucharist and the Mass. This made me more at peace, and I played better.

Eventually, later in the season, I was back in the starting lineup, but more deeply connected to, and centered on, Christ. I was more peaceful and centered in pressure situations because I was playing with, in, and for Christ, rather than for myself. It was a turning point that could have only occurred through failure, disappointment, and the carrying of a cross that opened me to a whole new and deeper faith perspective.

Crisis can lead to conversion, and my athletic crisis — as small as it was in ordinary terms — led to my internal conversion and prepared me for the rich experience of Princeton basketball.

The Princeton Basketball Experience, Coach Pete Carril, Spiritual Director Fr. James Halligan, and the Cosmic Power of the Catholic Mass

My three years playing junior varsity basketball at Princeton from 1978-1981 (I went up to the WPRB broadcast booth as an announcer my senior year) were exciting and deeply formational at every level.

As I was growing up, Princeton basketball always had a certain mystique for me. I watched legendary Princeton Rhodes Scholar Bill Bradley on the 1969-70 NBA Championship Knicks and heard radio announcer Marv Albert say from the Garden: "Frazier to Bradley. Bradley, side jump, YES!"

I read John McPhee's book, *A Sense of Where You Are*, on Bradley's Princeton career. I also remember, as a ninth grader, watching Princeton's run of upsets in the 1975 National Invitational Tournament at Madison Square Garden and seeing Coach Pete Carril and his players celebrate on the court after their final victory over Providence. I was mesmerized by an Ivy League team finishing the season at number 12 in the country. Little did I know, watching the Madison Square Garden celebration as a ninth grader, that Coach Pete Carril would one day become a friend and mentor.

Our JV coaches taught us Princeton basketball well. At the JV level, we were playing for pure love of the game, since we played in front of about 50-200 people and at times helped to prepare the varsity for their weekend games.

I had always enjoyed fast break basketball, and my speed and endurance made me effective at that style of play. But Princeton basketball was a whole new experience, involving a slower, possession-style offense. It is a beautiful blend of the building up and execution of fundamentals, such as precise chest passes (which raise shooting percentages), the setting up and timing behind effective picks, and the timing and execution of backdoor cuts and layups. To this day, Princeton basketball is an art form that involves intuitional team chemistry built on the foundation of sharply-honed fundamentals and radical unselfishness.

My academic work and playing at Jadwin Gym were connected to the daily Mass I attended with fellow Princetonians at 12:10 p.m. in Marquand Transept in the University Chapel. Mysteriously, I was living the sacrificial cosmic power of the Mass as I lived the sacrificial dimension of both my academic life and Princeton basketball.

Just as the aggressive basketball coaching at Princeton was helping to expand my character, leadership, and an understanding of how to promote team chemistry, I took on another critical coach — my spiritual director, Fr. James Halligan. He was stationed at Our Lady of Victory Parish on William Street in New York City, and I would take the train in to see him for spiritual direction every couple of weeks.

Father Halligan was radiant with holiness and listened to me during spiritual direction with a compassionate and contemplative focus. He listened the way that Christ would have listened, which encouraged me to tell him about everything I had experienced in life.

He had experienced many serious and life-threatening health problems for many years. His humble embrace of the Cross resulted in exceptional pastoral insight and receptivity to the gift of wisdom from the Holy Spirit, allowing the Spirit to work so humbly, gently, and powerfully in his priesthood. He had the most insight into human nature of any human being whom I have ever met.

At the end of the sessions, after I went to Confession, he would coach me about praying the Mass and the Rosary, meditating on Scripture, connecting to God with spiritual reading, and witnessing to my Catholic faith with a missionary spirit. He was gentle and compassionate, but as demanding as our basketball coaches at Jadwin Gym. The Holy Spirit used Fr. Halligan's spiritual direction — his pastoral insight, as well as his gentle and compassionate spirit — to begin forming me, especially my future pastoral charity and presence as a priest and bishop.

Sometimes it is only with the passage of time and deep prayer that the Holy Spirit gently reveals how different dimensions of your life have fit together. On February 24, 2007, Princeton University asked me, as a member of the Class of 1982's 25th reunion, to deliver the homily at the Princeton Service of Remembrance on Alumni Day at the University Chapel.

It was a unique opportunity to reflect on the spiritual, academic, and athletic dimensions of the Princeton experience as a Catholic priest. Here is a section from that homily, addressed to Princeton alumni of all ages in a packed University Chapel:

> But a *Service of Remembrance* is not only about the past. Remembering past Princetonians reminds us of what is important in the present. C.S. Lewis once

said that the men and women who end up being most productive in life are those who keep their eyes on Eternity.

Similarly, St. Ignatius of Loyola in his *Spiritual Exercises* encourages us to meditate on the scene of our own death bed. The purpose is to discern what exactly would be important to us at that moment. With that insight, we then project those priorities back into the present moment of our lives to enrich and deepen them. A *Service of Remembrance* helps us to do that. Our presence here shows that we want to do it.

Another way that a *Service of Remembrance* anchors us in the present is by evoking the living memories of our own Princeton experience that continue to influence us today. These memories will be as diverse as we are. But they are united in their impact on our lives. I share with you now some of my memories to help rekindle some of your own.

A senior thesis with Professor T.P. Roche focused on T.S. Eliot's transition from agnosticism to faith, as seen in his plays. Professor Joseph Frank's blend of history, biography, and literary criticism in his Dostoevsky seminar helped me to understand how the Russian novelist "came to faith through the furnace of doubt."

Professor Paul Ramsay's Christian Ethics course helped prepare me to read the encyclicals of Pope John Paul II. Intensive French grammar with Professor Andre Maman and a 19th-century French novel course with Professor Victor Brombert eventually led to a doctoral dissertation in Rome on the 17th century French School of spirituality.

Three years of JV basketball developed an appreciation of precise passing and backdoor cuts. It also reinforced a conviction that effective leadership and team play flow from sacrifice and selflessness.

And what an inspiration to watch Coach Carril bring Princeton basketball to the NBA (Coach Carril was an assistant coach for the Sacramento Kings after finishing at Princeton in 1996)!

Preparing this homily for a very diverse group of Princeton alumni of all ages helped me to trace the arc of God's providence working in my life through the Princeton experience in a way that resonated with other Princetonians. Little did I know how that arc would further expand just two years later, when Pope Benedict XVI appointed me to be the new bishop of the Diocese of Allentown.

The Spirituality of Sports and my Life as a Priest and Bishop

My background in sports made a significant difference in my life as a young parish priest. I always had a good arm for throwing a football, and in my first assignment, I was quickly nicknamed "Father Elway," after Super Bowl Champion quarterback John Elway, who was legendary for how far and how accurately he could throw downfield. Throwing footballs helped to break the ice and allowed me to talk about not only sports but spirituality as well with younger parishioners.

In my second assignment, we had great basketball games with the fathers of our school students and the students themselves. They were not always used to seeing young priests who were former college basketball players capable of hitting the 22-foot jump shot from the top of the key and threading the needle on a backdoor pass. The games were not only fun and great exercise for the adults, but they opened up many doors of practical evangelization with the families in the parish and school.

When Bishop Michael Saltarelli sent me to study in Rome as a graduate student priest, I played basketball at the North American College seminary on Tuesday afternoons with the seminarians, many of whom have become seminary rectors and priest leaders in their dioceses, and are still my friends. We enjoyed not only the games and the relief from academic stress that came from the exercise, but the fraternity and camaraderie of being among others who had similar interests. It was a practical lesson of how sports and spirituality can combine.

As the fourth bishop of the Diocese of Allentown, I often talked with young people about playing Princeton basketball. I usually told them that one of the ways the Holy Spirit prepared me to be a point guard in the Catholic Church as their bishop was by leading me to be a JV point guard at Princeton. I talked to them about my athletic crisis and Christ-centered conversion on the Andover varsity basketball team.

As a newly ordained bishop in 2009, I had the equivalent of a baseball card made. On one side is my picture as a bishop, and on the other side is a picture of me as a Princeton JV player at Jadwin Gym, going above the rim for a layup. I know that if, as a CYO basketball player, I had seen a picture of a priest or bishop playing college basketball and rising above the rim, it would have made a profound impression on me.

In the academic year 2009-2010, I gave a copy of that card personally to each of our Catholic elementary school students. All these years later, students still come up, remind me about the card, and tell me that they keep it on the bulletin board above their desk or carry it in their knapsack.

One of my favorite stories involves meeting the mother of a seventh grade boy who installed the card on his bedroom wall between posters of Michael Jordan and LeBron James. We had a great laugh together over that, and I laughed even more later when I imagined myself being dunked on, "posterized," and "facebookfriended" by Michael and LeBron simultaneously on that wall!

One of Princeton's legendary shooters, Frank Sowinski, "the Polish Rifle," said that the card was the best marketing for the priesthood he had ever seen. Speaking publicly about my vocation to the priesthood, I tell young people that just as Peter, James, and John were called by Christ from fishing nets, I was in many ways called by Christ to be a priest from the Princeton University Jadwin Gym basketball court. You could even say I was called from the nets hanging under the rims of the hoops to the spiritual nets that draw human beings into the barque of Peter, the Catholic Church.

In addition to the card, I conducted a basketball clinic focused on both basketball fundamentals and Catholic faith that we filmed. It has received around 9,000 hits on YouTube. I trust that it has done a lot of good, not just from a basketball point of view, but from a faith one, too.

Bishop Joseph McFadden and Bishop John Barres: Brother Bishops and Brother Point Guards

On May 8, 2013, I had the great privilege of preaching the funeral homily of my close friend Bishop Joseph McFadden, a priest of the Archdiocese of Philadelphia who became the bishop of the Diocese of Harrisburg, Pennsylvania.

I can still see us laughing outside of St. Charles Borromeo seminary planning some time together and then the very next morning hearing that he had died suddenly.

I can summarize our friendship and episcopal fraternity in a section from the homily that I delivered at his funeral that describes the conversations we had on the impact of the basketball experience on our Catholic faith and on our episcopal leadership:

> The young Joseph McFadden was an excellent student and the valedictorian of his St. Thomas More High School Class.
>
> He also experienced early on what many metro Philadelphia boys have experienced through the generations — a love for Big Five basketball, triple-headers at the Palestra, and the Philadelphia Catholic League.
>
> I can remember one of my own mentors, legendary Princeton basketball coach Pete Carril, saying that he liked to recruit Catholic High School players because "they play to win."

Make no mistake about it. Joseph McFadden may have been a kind and gentle priest and bishop but he always played to win — whether it was a West Catholic game or whether it was the New Evangelization!

And his way to win as a priest and bishop with a rich interior life and a vibrant missionary spirit was a non-stop full court press for the Glory of God and the salvation of souls.

So many of his basketball experiences, first as a point guard and then as a coach at West Catholic, forged his style of priestly and episcopal leadership.

As a point guard initiating the offense, passing the ball, and creating team chemistry, he would survey the floor, see a lane, and then go very hard to the basket.

It was the same dynamic for him as a bishop of the New Evangelization. He would survey the challenges of spreading the Gospel in the 21st century age of social networking, moral relativism, hedonism and radical atheism.

Then he would find that lane of opportunity, and he would go to the basket hard with a constructive strategy, plan of action, and a spirit of winning and contagious enthusiasm. He was relentless in the best sense.

At the same time, he had this calm, listening, and engaging pastoral spirit that focused prayerfully on the person God put in front of him at a particular moment.

Blessed John Paul II captures Bishop McFadden's spirit in a passage from his book on his life as a bishop entitled *Rise, Let Us Be on Our Way.* He writes: "Interest in others begins with the bishop's prayer life: his conversations with Christ, who entrusts 'His own' to him. Prayer prepares him for encounter with others ... I simply pray for everyone every day.

As soon as I meet people, I pray for them, and this helps me in all my relationships ... I always follow this principle: I welcome everyone as a person sent to me and entrusted to me by Christ."

Bishop McFadden lived this spirit daily. In the wide range of people he touched and influenced, he welcomed everyone as a person sent and entrusted to him by Christ Himself.

May my friend, brother bishop, and brother point guard rest in peace! He is a daily inspiration.

Final Thoughts

On January 27, 2016, I spoke to the Alvernia University men's basketball team right before they took the floor and said these words:

The older I get, the more I realize how formative the basketball experience is for you later in life. You put in a lot of hard work and sacrifice on your shooting, ball handling, speed, and court awareness. The development of team chemistry, sacrifice, and generosity — seeing the big picture over the course of a season — is so key to your future career paths, your future marriages and families. There is one thing I want to leave you with tonight: Put Christ at the center of your basketball experience and the development of selfless team chemistry. Play basketball for the glory of God. Be Christ-driven and glory-of-God-driven on the court rather than ego-driven, and our Lord will take your experience of the game of basketball to a whole other beautiful and inspirational level that will impact your destiny and future contributions to the Church and to the world.

I spoke these words from my personal experience of the Holy Spirit leading, guiding, and forming me through the game of basketball. I spoke them from my heart and pastoral experience as a priest and bishop.

I hope that they took root in the souls of those college basketball players who were present. I also hope that they will take root in the souls of those who read this chapter so they might consider striving to lead lives that are not driven by ego but are instead driven by Christ, the glory of God, and the universal call to holiness and mission. They will find that doing so is the key to happiness and fulfillment in this life and eternal life with Christ in the next.

The major concern of a Catholic bishop is to surrender, as a successor of the apostles, to the Holy Spirit in being an instrument for helping to lead souls to Heaven. This became even clearer to me when our Holy Father Pope Francis sent me to be the fifth bishop of the Diocese of Rockville Centre, New York, where I was installed on January 31, 2017. Being an "apostolic athlete" for the New Evangelization is a joy and inspiration, and I hope that all those under my spiritual care will participate in the victory celebration with the saints in Heaven.

Father Rocha with 5-time MLB All-Star Mike Sweeney

FATHER
RICHARD ROCHA

Coaching God's People to the Ultimate Goal

THE DATE WAS OCTOBER 27, 2015. The whole country was ready to watch Game 1 of the Major League Baseball World Series. I never thought that not only would I be sitting in Kauffman Stadium as this happened, but that I would be sitting there as the Catholic chaplain for the Kansas City Royals. I have often looked back on my life and seen God's mighty hand guiding me, giving me these wonderful opportunities to experience the thrill of sports. This thrill has drawn and characterized me for most of my life.

I have frequently contemplated "the call" of our Lord to me to enter seminary in pursuit of the Catholic priesthood. Answering this call meant leaving behind a passion, a deep desire to do something that I truly felt comfortable doing, which was coaching football. It was a difficult decision for me to give up something that I had felt was my vocation — teaching young men how to be winners on and off the field.

I was born in Atchison, Kansas, and was the third of Robert and Mary Rocha's five children. We grew up in St. Joseph, Missouri, and our parents were very devout, faith-filled models of Catholicism for us. They believed in Catholic education and made sure that we attended Catholic grade school and high school. I remember sitting in the second grade classroom at St. Patrick Grade School. Our associate pastor would occasionally come in and talk with us about a vocation to the priesthood and/or the religious life. I would often raise my hand when Father would ask if any of us boys would like to become a priest.

This occurred for a few years until fifth grade. It was then that the religious sisters teaching us received all sorts of playground equipment from the Knights of Columbus. When I saw that football rolling out of the bag, it was almost like a magnet that attached itself to me. The sisters only let us play football on Fridays, since we had an asphalt playground that often did a number on our pants and shirts. After that, Father would enter our classroom and begin with the same routine, talking about vocations. However, this time I remember literally sitting on my hands to make sure that I didn't raise either of them. I was convinced that I wanted my life to include football in a special and unique way.

I was able to play football in junior high school, in preparation for attending Bishop LeBlond Catholic High School in order to play for a legendary coach in our area, Don Tabor. I learned a great deal from him, and my desire and hard work earned me a scholarship to play football at the college level. Benedictine College was not only the *alma mater* of my high school coach, but is located in my birthplace.

I played there for two years and had really worked hard to learn everything I could, knowing that I wanted to continue my life as a teacher and a coach. After my sophomore year at Benedictine was finished, my father suddenly died in June. It was a total shock to our family. Suddenly I felt torn between continuing on at Benedictine and coming home to the town of St. Joseph to finish my degree in education at Missouri Western State University. Coach Tabor quickly became a father figure to me and helped me settle my decision. He wanted me to come and help him coach at LeBlond, and suggested that I finish my degree.

I began my coaching career at the age of 20, and although I still struggled to deal with the death of my father, I remember how "natural" it felt being on the field as a football coach. My desire to be molded by Coach Tabor served me well on and off the field, as he helped me start to truly embrace my faith. My mother and father had set great examples for us, showing us how to always put God first in our lives and draw close to Our Blessed Mother, knowing that she would only lead us closer to her Son, Jesus. Mom was a daily communicant until she had to go to work after my father's death, and I quickly learned more about how important Holy Mass was to Coach Tabor, as he attended daily as well.

One Thursday night, I was watching film with Coach Tabor in preparation for a game the next night. I remember him asking me if I wanted to meet him at Mass the next day, and that it was a First Friday. This was an invitation I sometimes received from my mother, but now it was coming from this coaching legend. I quickly responded "yes" to Coach Tabor and remembered that Mass started at 7 a.m. This wasn't a pleasant thought, but I got up in time, anyhow. I was definitely the youngest person at Mass by many years, so I was out of place in that respect, but after it was over, I thought to myself that it wasn't so bad after all.

I started to go to Mass each Friday with Coach Tabor before football games. Later on, before the start of Lent, my promise was to go to Mass one day each week during the Lenten season. This quickly became a habit, and led to me attending Mass each day during Lent. I was being drawn to the Holy Eucharist and started to have the desire to receive our Lord in Holy Communion each day, like the desire experienced by my own mother and my high school coach. This change in my life quickly led me to embrace the Sacrament of Confession and seek it out more frequently. This was due to Coach Tabor, who, after some slip-ups of mine, would be on the phone to Msgr. Summers to tell him that I would be coming to see him for Confession.

My love for the game and experience in coaching helped cultivate my desire to coach on the college level and also work to obtain my master's degree in education. I was hired as a graduate assistant football coach at Northwest Missouri State University in Maryville, Missouri. I continued to attend daily Mass and would often run into my academic advisor, Dr. Jim Redd, there as well. Dr. Redd (former head football coach at Northwest) and I became fast friends and it was such a blessing to have him as a mentor.

I was in my fourth month at Northwest and remember talking with Fr. Don Miller, a senior priest in residence at St. Gregory, after Mass. He said, "You're one of the new coaches up at the University, right?" I replied, "Yes, Father, I am." He said, "I see you here at daily mass." I said, "Yes, I even got the head coach, who is Methodist, to change our meeting time to 8:45 a.m. so I can come to 8 a.m. Mass!" He said, "Have you ever thought about the priesthood?" I replied, "Oh no, Father; I'm a football coach." He never once asked me again but as I look back on that conversation, it was definitely a seed that was being planted.

I enjoyed my two years at Northwest, and my knowledge of football continued to expand as I spent the next two years coaching on the collegiate level. My love for daily Mass continued to grow, and I often found myself making sacrifices of my time in order to keep this commitment. I started to realize that my faith life could fit in very well with my coaching career, as Coach Tabor had made very clear. I was being formed into a disciple for Christ, and no longer living the life of "do as I say, not as I do."

It was now time to continue my pursuit of a career coaching football; I also had the desire to be a head football coach. There was a small high school team not far from the city of St. Joseph that had struggled for the past three years. North Platte had won two games the previous three years, and I remember thinking that there should be only one way to go with this team. After being hired by the school board, I held a team meeting shortly after the school year let out. I also extended an invitation to the parents and the alumni, telling them I was happy to be a part of this program, and that they could expect discipline, hard work, and commitment.

I explained my philosophy that I had played under and was now adopting as my own as a coach. It was the 3-F philosophy. I shared with the men that first and foremost in their life should be their FAITH. We will not make it in this challenging world unless we have faith in God, who should be at the center of our lives. Next in my philosophy was FAMILY. I shared with the team and the others gathered there about having a deep respect and love for their parents and siblings, explaining that family is a building block to faith. I shared with them that last in the philosophy was FOOTBALL. Football is often number one in the life of a coach, but it would not be number one for me. I think I recall some of the parents and alumni talking about getting ready for another three years with a record of 2-28, but I held to this philosophy each day of my head coaching career and was able to see it make an impact on the players.

In my first year at North Platte, we won two games. The people of the community thought that I was the best thing since sliced bread. The next two years had us winning five games and nine games respectively, taking the conference championship and making it all the way to the quarterfinals in state competition.

I look back on those first three years of my experience as a head coach and realize how important the 3-F philosophy is in the life of a young man. I recently got on Facebook and friended some of my former athletes. One particular young man shared this with me in a message: "Good morning Father (and forever to me 'Coach') Rocha. Thank you for accepting my friend request. I can't believe it's been 20 years since I last talked with you at North Platte. You were my first true mentor and role model and, whether you knew it or not, [you] helped mold me into the man, husband, father, and firefighter I am today. I just wanted to say thank you. God bless." I realized how important it was for me to develop this philosophy and watch how it affected these young men.

The success at North Platte inspired me to venture out and see what other coaching opportunities might be out there. At the time, I wondered why I didn't stay there; why would I want to leave? I was half an hour from my family and friends, which brought me much comfort. It was a program that won the State Championship two years later under the direction one of my former assistants.

During the spring of 1996, I was offered a job at a bigger school in southern Missouri, Mount Vernon High School. It was a 3A school that had also been struggling the previous three seasons. I took this job on with the same sort of passion and desire that I had brought to the North Platte position. But being four hours away from home and in an area where there were very few Catholics brought on some extra challenges. I look back on that experience now and realized how this allowed me to discern more deeply God's will in my life without the comforts of family, friends, and home.

There was a Catholic church in town just half a mile from the high school, which allowed me to continue going to daily Mass. I quickly became friends with the pastor, Msgr. John Westhues, who provided great spiritual guidance. I remember not being able to sleep at night and thought God was calling me to a deeper spiritual life. I started coming earlier for Mass and spending time in front of the Blessed Sacrament, thinking that this was the direction that God was indicating for me. The more time I spent with our Lord, the more confused I seemed to become, if that makes any sense. I started questioning whether I should be in this town and high school, and more importantly, if I should even be coaching football. I would then quickly revert back to the mindset of my younger years, when football was everything to me, and wonder why I would be questioning anything now.

It was October of 1996, and after daily Mass, I remember walking into the sacristy and asking Msgr. Westhues if he had some time to visit. I called the high school and let them know that I would not be there for first hour class. Monsignor and I sat down and had a cup of coffee. I explained to him that I hadn't been able to sleep at night and was a little confused about God and where He might be calling me. I shared that I didn't know if I was supposed to be coaching at Mount Vernon, or even coaching and teaching at all. Monsignor quickly calmed me down and wanted me to speak a bit about my spiritual life. I first spoke about my love for daily Mass and receiving our Lord in Holy Communion each day, and how I didn't know what I would do if I couldn't receive Him each day. I expressed my love for the other Sacraments, especially the Sacrament of Confession. I went on and on with great joy and comfort in speaking about my faith and my desire to be married and have a family. But then he asked the question, "Coach, are you sure God's not calling you to the priesthood?"

I remember tears welling up in my eyes and my face falling into my hands. I looked up at Monsignor and said, "Monsignor, maybe He is, but I don't think I want to be a priest! I want to coach football and get married and have a huge family." Wisely, this older priest offered me two great pieces of advice. He said, "Coach, first of all, have you ever asked God what He has in store for you?" I quickly thought over my life and answered, "No, Monsignor. I guess I really haven't prayed about what His will would be for me. I guess I simply prayed that He bless my journey, and I have been doing what I have wanted to do since grade school."

Monsignor suggested, "First of all, each day, pray to God and ask what His will is for you. Ask what His 'call' is for you today, and ask that you have the strength and courage to do His will. Then follow it up with three Hail Marys. Second, don't rule out 'marriage' in His 'call' for you, because God wants good, strong men to be 'married' to His Church, and to be 'fathers' to His people." It hit me like a lightning bolt, and a big weight was lifted off my shoulders. I realized that I could still have this desire to be a husband and father, but also keep asking God what vocation He has for me.

After continued visits with Msgr. Westhues and much prayer, I realized that God was not calling me to coach football. He was calling me to "coach" on *His* team. I remember heading home to St. Joseph for winter break, the whole time trying to figure out how I was going to spring this on my mother. When I arrived home to St. Joseph, one of my sisters said that someone needed to go to Atchison, Kansas, and pick up Mom. Mom, who was one of 13 children, was there visiting with her sisters. I quickly jumped at the opportunity and thought, "Great opportunity to tell Mom ... and if she faints or has a heart attack, I'll just drive her straight to the hospital."

I arrived at my aunt's house and remember how the conversation quickly turned to me. They asked how the new job was going, if there was a Catholic church in town and if I was going to it, and if I had met any young women to date. I replied that it was going well and "yes" to the rest of the questions. I remember one of my aunts saying, "Good, you can start settling down and get married and start your family!" It was then that my mother spoke up and said, "Oh, no, Richie's the one that I've been praying to be my priest!"

My jaw dropped, and the only thing that I remember next was saying, "Mom, are you ready to go?"

We said our goodbyes and left for St. Joseph. I remember driving over the Amelia Earhart Bridge into Missouri and pulling off to the side of the road. Mom asked what was wrong, and I said, "Mom, why did you say that?" She responded, "Say what?" I said, "Why did you say that you've been praying that I be your priest?" She said that ever since I started coaching (I was then in my 14th year of it) that she "had been praying a novena to Our Lady of Guadalupe and St. Jude, that God would call you to the priesthood." With our Hispanic heritage, I could see why she'd be praying to Our Lady of Guadalupe, but said, "Mom, why St. Jude?" She replied, "Because he's the patron saint of hopeless cases! I figured it would be hard, since you love football so much." I told her that this is why I was the one to pick her up in Atchison. After she asked why, I said, "Mom, I think God is calling me to the priesthood, and I feel called to enter seminary formation and find out if this is His will for me."

I think 14 years of tears came out of my mom's eyes. I remember asking her how come she never tried to talk me

Father Rocha with his mother, Mary

into it after all these years. She replied, "I wanted it to be your decision, and I never missed a day praying that novena for you!" No wonder she added St. Jude to the lineup of intercessors. We had such an emotional trip back home, and then I said, "Ok, now how are we going to tell the rest of the family?"

It was in the fall of 1997 that I entered my first year at Mundelein

Seminary in a northern suburb of Chicago, Illinois. I was truly blessed along the way to stay somewhat close to football and sports. Carmel Catholic High School was located across the street from the seminary. I was asked by their football coach to help out just a few days a week. I thought about it for a long time and asked the seminary rector, Fr. John Canary, if this would be possible. He suggested that I concentrate on my studies, instead. Thanks be to God he said, "No."

I also attended my first Notre Dame football game that year, and met a gentleman from my home town of St. Joseph. He was a graduate of Bishop LeBlond and also played football under Coach Tabor about nine years before I did. He now lived in South Bend, Indiana, and provided me with tickets to home football games at Notre Dame.

After my second year of theology, I was asked by the seminary rector to coach our basketball team. I remember saying, "Father Canary, I've never coached basketball!" His reply was somewhat comforting, saying that it shouldn't be too hard for someone who had coached all those years. I thank God that I still had connections with some of my coaching buddies from my former high schools to help me get the basics down.

I enjoyed my formation at Mundelein, but it was rocky at first. I failed my first philosophy test and remember the professor saying that if I struggled with his class, then theology would be very difficult for me, as well. I thought that was my ticket home. I would return to coaching football and teaching, but after my visit to the chapel, I ran into Fr. Pat Boyle. Father Boyle saw me pass his office and invited me in. His first question to me was, "Are you the football coach?" I remember smiling at him, clutching my fist around my test paper, and saying, "Yes, and maybe that's what God still wants me to do." I explained to him about my first test and remember him saying, "So … you're going to quit after one failed test? I hope you didn't coach football that way!" We quickly struck up a friendship, and he later became my spiritual father throughout the rest of my seminary years. I struck up many friendships with other seminarians, most of whom had some type of athletic background. I remember this helping solidify my call by allowing me to see that God wants ordinary men to be His "coaches" in His Church.

I was ordained to the priesthood in the Diocese of Kansas City-St. Joseph by Bishop Raymond Boland on June 1, 2002, at St. Elizabeth Parish in Kansas City, Missouri. I have been a parochial vicar, parish administrator, pastor, priest secretary and master of ceremonies to the bishop, director of vocations for the Diocese of Kansas City-St. Joseph, and am presently the president of St. Michael the Archangel High School. I also currently serve as the Catholic chaplain for the Kansas City Royals and Kansas City Chiefs (via my involvement with Catholic Athletes for Christ).

I had been worried that by leaving my duties as a football coach, I would be deprived of something very good, and that I might never actually be happy if I became a priest. However, the opposite is true: By "leaving" football and going after what God wanted for me, I have truly "found" football and so many other sports. My coaching duties have not gone away; they have simply expanded and become more profound. Now the final goal is "coaching" people to get to Heaven.

Father Benander with Cardinal Raymond Burke

FATHER ALAN BENANDER, O PRAEM

'Senior Rookie of the Year' Perseveres to Previously Unexpected Heights

IT WAS JUNE 22, 2013, and I knelt down in front of the altar at the Mission Basilica San Juan Capistrano (in San Juan Capistrano, California) as the bishop, His Excellency Kevin Vann, pronounced the words of priestly ordination over my confrere Fr. Nathanial Drogin, O Praem, and me, making us priests of Jesus Christ forever. This is a moment that will forever be etched in my mind. "I'm a priest!"

I remember thinking, as I looked down at my hands in joyful shock, that from that moment on, by the power of this priestly ordination, I, with these hands and the words of consecration, would be able to turn mere bread into the Body of Christ. I could hardly believe it — and I can still hardly believe it! I was, and am, a priest! It was an unbelievably joyful moment — a moment filled, not with just any joy, but with a truly profound, deep joy that lasts to this day and, I am quite sure, will remain with me forever.

In some ways, it was sports that helped lead me to the altar that day to be ordained, since it was in sports that I learned many important life lessons, lessons that have led me to become a priest (and lessons that, I hope and pray, will help me to be a good and faithful priest). The lessons that I learned by playing sports included how to work well with others, overcome adversity, and strive for high goals — all lessons that every man who is to become a priest must learn in order to fulfill his priestly role well.

Born on November 26, 1976, the fourth of eight children (five girls and three boys), in a suburb of Cleveland, Ohio, I began to play (and to follow) sports at a young age. My father was a high school baseball and hockey coach, and so he naturally passed on his knowledge and love of baseball to me and my siblings. While I enjoyed playing and following all sports — everyone in my family was, and still is, a huge fan of the Cleveland sports teams — it was baseball that eventually became my favorite sport, and the one that I took most seriously.

My father often told me, "Practice makes perfect." So, taking those words to heart, I worked hard to try to become a good baseball player. With the aid of the batting cage that

Dad and I built in our backyard, I really devoted myself to becoming a good hitter. In due time, with lots of practice, coaching from Dad and others (e.g., my Uncle Al), and playing lots of baseball in the backyard with my brother John and our friends, I did develop some skill at playing the game. I was consistently one of the better players in whatever league I played in all throughout my grade school years. At some point, I, like many other American boys, began to dream of being a big league ball player; this dream is what really motivated me to work hard at the game to achieve my goal of being a professional ball player.

I went to St. Ignatius High School, a Jesuit school in Cleveland — a top-notch sports school as well as a top-ranked school academically — and, I might add, a school that did a good job of instilling in me a greater knowledge and love of our Lord and our Catholic faith. While St. Ignatius' sports program was (and still is) known most especially for its excellent football program (three national titles and the school with the most state titles in football-rich Ohio, including four in my four years there), when I arrived at St. Ignatius in 1991, the school was also beginning to develop an excellent baseball program. Therefore, when I entered St. Ignatius, I was very excited to try to be a part of a team that could perhaps be the first to win a baseball state title for our school.

Soon after baseball practice began in my freshman year, I knew that we had a good team; indeed, early on, I knew that we had enough talent to make a legitimate run at a state title, if we but put in the work needed to do so. This is one of the excellent lessons I learned in sports: the necessity of working hard alongside other boys/men in order to achieve a lofty goal — in this case, trying to win a state baseball championship. In my freshman year, our team performed well, and I also did well personally, with the dream of playing professionally still strong in my mind.

This success continued into my sophomore year, although at the time I was rather disappointed not to be playing varsity ball. Nevertheless I regrouped from that disappointment and put together perhaps the best season of my life. My teammates and I enjoyed a 19-0 record on the junior varsity team. Having my dad as the head JV baseball coach that year also made the season very special. I would not trade it for anything, even a chance to play varsity as a sophomore. I learned some good lessons in this JV season: In addition to continuing to learn the value of team camaraderie, I also learned how to deal with adversity (in this case, dealing with not being called up to varsity as I was hoping) by being optimistic and "mentally tough." (I should note that, on this point, I was aided by reading an excellent book called *Mental Toughness Training for Sports* by James Loehr.)

These lessons continued for me in the latter years of high school, as I moved on to the varsity team in pursuit of the school's first baseball title — and in pursuit of my dream of being a pro ball player. In my junior year, I first needed to learn how to deal with the disappointment of not being in the starting line-up or getting as much playing time as I had hoped I would (and thought I deserved). Yet rather than allowing this to affect me too much, I worked hard the following summer on my game and came back my senior year ready to play some ball.

However, I was faced with more adversity when, to my (and at least some of my teammates') surprise, I was not in the starting line-up at the beginning of that season, either. Again, I tried not to let this get to me and waited for my chance to break into the line-up. Eventually, I was given that chance. I got some clutch pinch-hits in pressure situations and won the starting job at first base. I worked my way into the heart of the batting order and by season's end, I was leading our team in batting average. This was a very exciting time: I was a key member of a top-ranked, very talented team (a team that included one future big leaguer and a number of future Division I college players). I was very proud to be a part of this team, and I was performing rather well heading into the playoffs.

However, it was at this point that God gave me what was perhaps the greatest sports-related adversity in my life. In the last regular season game of my senior year, facing our archrival, St. Edward High School of Cleveland, and playing well in that game, I broke my ankle sliding into second base trying to break up a double play. This mishap ended my season and knocked me out of the playoffs — the playoffs I had dreamed of playing in ever since my freshman year at St. Ignatius. This was heart-breaking.

With my good mother by my side in the doctor's office, I shed tears when the announcement came that my ankle was broken, knowing that my dream of battling with my teammates for a state title was, in one instant, shattered. Oh, eventually I, with my crutches, joined my teammates on the bench to cheer them on as they continued the fight for the title. I was happy that my replacement at first base (a great athlete who would later play in the NFL) did perform very well, including hitting a game-winning homerun.

In the end, the team went far, but fell just short in their efforts to win our school a baseball crown, losing to the eventual champions in the semifinal game. All this — not playing in the playoffs and our team falling just short of that lofty goal for which we had striven for four years — was quite difficult to endure. These were crosses given to me through sports, experiences that also gave me good lessons on my road to the priesthood, for a priest is a man who must learn to endure and love the Cross.

After high school, I went to John Carroll University, a Division III school in Cleveland. The lessons I learned in baseball at JCU were, I believe, very important for me on my journey to the priesthood. The first lesson I learned was humility. As I headed to JCU, I just assumed that I would be given a spot on the baseball team. I had performed well for a highly-ranked high school team, and I had also been recruited by JCU's previous coach to play baseball there. However, for multiple reasons, I did not really have my heart in the game during tryouts. As a result, my performance suffered greatly, and I was cut from JCU my freshman year by the new coach.

This was a great humiliation, since I had always seen myself playing Division I college baseball somewhere. To get cut from a Division III team was unthinkable. It was more of the same my sophomore year when I once again tried out for the JCU team: I still did not really have my heart in the game. I was plagued with some injuries, and I had difficulties getting over the disappointment of not being able to play at a Division I college, so I performed well below my potential and, in the end, got cut again.

By my junior year, however, I was starting to get my heart back into the game. Perhaps it was a side effect of being out of scholastic ball for two years. Perhaps it was the result of realizing (and being excited about) the challenge of trying to make the team after being cut two times already. I went into those tryouts with more determination and heart than I had the previous two tryouts. As a result, I performed well; well enough, I thought, to make the team. However, the coach, having already seen me perform poorly in the previous two tryouts, did not keep me. I got cut for the third time — another humiliation.

Still, having recalled my previous lofty goals for baseball (that is, to be a pro ball player), I was determined to make the team for JCU, so I tried out again my senior year. Some people thought I was crazy for doing so, but I played extremely well in these tryouts. At one point, rumors were flying that not only would I make the team, but that I would be the starting third baseman. Yet at the end of tryouts, I got cut — *initially*. However, to my shock, the coach inexplicably changed his mind. I believe a prayer I made in front of the Blessed Sacrament may have had something to do with his change of heart;

as Proverbs 21:1 says, "The heart of the king [or in this case, the coach!] is in the hand of the Lord."

So after four years and getting cut three times, I was *finally* on the team. I performed pretty well — doing fine in the field and hitting over .350 that season, earning "Rookie of the Year" honors from my coach and teammates as a senior! The previous years' humiliations made the eventual breakthrough onto the team — not to mention doing pretty well that year on the field — that much sweeter. (This is also something that we Cleveland sports fans recently experienced, having faced 52 years of winning no championships in any sport until the Cavaliers' incredible NBA title in 2016; overcoming the 52-year "curse" made the title that much more glorious!) The humiliations I faced gave me occasions to exercise humility, perseverance, and endurance — other lessons that are important for a priest to learn.

After graduating from JCU, I went to work as a computer programmer at Progressive Corporation, a Cleveland-based auto insurance company. While I very much enjoyed my job at Progressive, I did not lose sight of my dream of playing professional baseball. I continued to stay in shape and played ball in the summer in the hopes of walking on to one of the teams in the Frontier League, an independent, semi-professional baseball league in the Midwest that has seen some players go to the big leagues. I knew that walking on to one of these teams at their open tryouts would be difficult, as only a small percentage of players at these sorts of tryouts are hired.

However, I believed there was a chance I could make one of these teams, so I worked hard — and I prayed hard — in order to fulfill my boyhood dream of playing at some level of professional ball. In the end, while I did perform well at these tryouts (one day I hit a double and a triple), I did not make a team. While I was not shocked about this, I was disappointed. After many years, my boyhood dream of playing pro ball had finally ended.

However, my lifelong efforts to make it in professional baseball were not wasted. By striving for this lofty goal, sports trained me to aim high — an important lesson for any Christian, especially a priest, to learn. Following the Frontier League tryouts, I wondered why my prayers to God in this regard did not result in me becoming a pro ballplayer. But in due time, I came to realize that God *had* listened to — and *would* answer — these prayers by giving me something *better* than becoming a pro baseball player: He would make me a priest! Indeed, I have always found that, whenever we ask God for something and He does not give us exactly what we want, He will, like the good Father that He is, give us something *better*.

Not long after this last ditch effort to make it as a baseball player, I encountered some very good friends in the St. Rose Young Adults Group in Cleveland. At the time I met this group, I thought that I had written off the priesthood as a possible state of life for me. Although I had given some thought to the priesthood in college, I believed it was not for me and was pursuing marriage, since I had always thought that I would find a good wife and have lots of children, like my own dad had done. But, through friendships with members of this group, especially with the head of this group, Eric, I really grew in my knowledge and love of the Catholic faith. With this came an increased appreciation for the priesthood. After much prayer and study about the priesthood, as well as a number of conversations with priests, I came to love the idea of becoming a priest.

In due time, with my aforementioned friend, Eric (who himself, at the time, was considering becoming a priest and who, more than anyone else at this time, encouraged and motivated me to consider the priesthood), I began visiting seminaries and religious communities and, in the end, discovered St. Michael's Abbey — an abbey of the Norbertine Order (Order of Prémontré) in Southern California. Although I had not previously heard of St. Michael's Abbey, or even of the Norbertine Order (nor of the heroic founder of the order, St. Norbert), I very quickly grew to love both the abbey and the order. The aspects of the abbey that really drew me to join included the abbey's fidelity to the Church and her traditions, both theological and liturgical (such as Gregorian chant, reverently celebrated Masses, the study of St. Thomas Aquinas and St. Augustine, and the wearing of the white Norbertine habit).

In addition to offering Mass in a reverent manner, the community named after St. Norbert, a great "apostle of the Eucharist," shows its devotion to the Blessed Sacrament through a daily Eucharistic Holy Hour); strong community life (with many young members); strong devotion to Our Lady (which is so very important for us priests); devotion to the Scriptures and *lectio divina;* and carrying out apostolic works to which I felt drawn — for example, working in schools and parishes.

So I entered the abbey on August 27, 2003 (the feast of St. Monica, mother of St. Augustine), and on Christmas Eve of that same year, I received from our abbot, Eugene Hayes, the white Norbertine habit and my religious name of "Alan" (after the great devotee of the Virgin Mary Blessed Alan de la Roche. "Alan" is also the name of my very good uncle and godfather, "Uncle Al"). I made my solemn vows on August 28, 2010, on the Feast of St. Augustine, one of our order's "holy fathers," as we follow his monastic rule; and was ordained a priest, as stated above, on June 22, 2013, the Feast of St. Thomas More and St. John Fisher.

When I entered the abbey, I did not know if, or to what extent, I would be involved in baseball and other sports as a member of the Order. I had been deeply involved in sports prior to entering, but I was willing to give all that up, if that is what our Lord willed. As our Lord would have it, not only have I had a chance to be involved in baseball and other sports in some special ways since entering, but in even more special ways than I probably ever would have if I had *not* entered. This shows that our Lord's words in chapter 19 of St. Matthew's Gospel are true — whatever we give up for our Lord will be returned one hundred-fold!

First of all, since entering St. Michael's Abbey, I have realized much more clearly than ever before the value that sports and exercise have for the development of one's *spiritual* life. I was helped to this realization by reading a good book on the topic, *The Catholic Ideal: Exercise and Sports* by Robert Feeney. The community sports at St. Michael's Abbey (which we engaged in often when I was in the seminary) built up the spirit of the community and helped keep us physically healthy — which, in turn, helped strengthen our minds and wills. I began to see more clearly how sports truly are a way to "glorify God in the body," as St. Paul exhorts us to do.

More than that, since entering St. Michael's, I have had wonderful opportunities to meet, work with, and form friendships with a number of former big league ballplayers, such as pitcher Justin Speier (who occasionally visits our abbey) and Mike Sweeney (whom I worked with at his Catholic Baseball Camp in San Diego). In addition, one of my confreres, Frater Matthew (Grant) Desme, was a star in the Oakland A's minor league system and had a very good chance of becoming a Major Leaguer, especially after winning the 2009 Arizona Fall League MVP award. But he gave up baseball to join our community, doing what the "rich young man" in the Gospel would not do by giving up worldly success to follow Christ more closely. This shocked the sports world, as well as my family and friends back in Cleveland, who marveled that, "of all places" a professional ballplayer would choose to enter, it would be the same community that I, a "baseball nut," had already entered! Frater Matthew's story has said many things to many people; for me, it confirmed for me that God, in calling me to the priesthood and to St. Michael's Abbey, had called me to something even better than the Major Leagues.

Through my association with these ballplayers since entering St. Michael's, I have had such memorable experiences as taking batting practice off a big leaguer, for Justin Speier was kind enough to pitch batting practice (BP) and run a baseball practice for me and my fellow seminarians a while ago. Although he was only pitching "BP speed" in that practice and though the fences were not very far, now I can say that I hit a homerun off a big leaguer! I was also able to pitch

BP to a big leaguer and a would-be big leaguer when I was the pitcher for a fun homerun derby contest between Mike Sweeney and Frater Matthew at the boys' summer camp which our abbey community runs every summer.

Furthermore, at St. Michael's Abbey, I have had a chance to coach high school baseball. Our abbey runs a high school, St. Michael's Preparatory School in Silverado, California, and I have been either an assistant or head coach for the team for several seasons, which I have very much enjoyed. I especially enjoyed last season, when I had the wonderful opportunity to coach with Frater Matthew, learning quite a bit about the game from him as we, along with another community member, Frater Vianney Ceja, coached the team to a league championship.

Most recently, I have had the special opportunity to offer Mass as a chaplain for both the Angels and the Dodgers. This afforded me the opportunity to meet some special baseball personalities who, more importantly, are faithful Catholics such as legendary Dodgers announcer Vin Scully and Los Angeles Angels manager Mike Scioscia.

All of these special baseball experiences have shown me that, though a priest must indeed elevate his mind to the things of Heaven and, in the process, have a certain amount of real detachment from the things of this world, including sports and baseball, there is still *some* role for sports and exercise in the life of a priest. God, being the good Father that He is, knows how much I love and benefit from baseball and other sports, so He has provided me with these sorts of special experiences. As stated above, these are part of the "hundred fold" that He has offered to me since I chose to follow Him more closely in the religious life and the priest-hood. Now, I just pray that I, for my part, will be a good son to Him and so make a gift of thanks to Him by using these experiences to become a better priest and lead more souls to Heaven, and so glorify Him — Father, Son, and Holy Spirit — in the process. Amen.

FATHER
GABRIEL LICKTEIG

Warming Up to the Lord

A THLETICS HAVE BEEN A HUGE part of my life as far back as I can remember. From a very young age there were always games to be played, particularly around our family's first house in northeast Kansas City. A group of about seven or eight boys who lived on our block, including my younger brother, were always mustering up something to play in the street or surrounding yards. By the grace of God, I possessed a natural aptitude for athletics, whether it was swinging a baseball bat, running around a basketball court, or kicking a soccer ball.

Like many young Catholic boys, I was heavily inspired by the sports culture, especially by movies like *Rudy*. When I was growing up, the "mega sports star" in Kansas City was Tony Gonzalez, one of the greatest tight ends to ever play the game of football. Gonzalez's posters adorned my room, and dreams of catching a 40-yard touchdown pass down the seam danced in my head.

My family's faith around this time could be called average: We attended Mass on Sundays, prayed before meals, and were involved in sports and school activities at St. Patrick's in Kansas City. Yet something was missing. The Catholic faith was not as exciting or important as the false idols of sports, human glory, and being known by others. In hindsight, you could say that the capacity I had been given for God alone was not being properly used or cared for. Instead, it was used to make idols of athletes and other famous people of this world. With those false gods governing my worldview, I carved out a plan for my life that I thought would fulfill me: Play professional sports, have a beautiful wife and kids, make lots of money, and ride off into the sunset.

When I was in grade school, my friends and I discovered that I had a natural gift for kicking footballs. I could boom the ball, and people would stand around and watch as the pigskin went soaring. During my junior year of high school, I parlayed that into becoming the starting punter. We had a truly amazing ride that year, winning the state championship. The following year, we didn't do so hot as a team, but I was still able to attain second team All-State and keep the dream of athletic glory alive. I had enough talent to keep the possibility open. During summers in high school, I attended kicking camps with other high school and college kickers from around the Midwest and took home the best punter award in camp at every camp I attended.

During one of the camps, while I was undergoing my final evaluation (consisting of 10 kicks), a then-active NFL punter told me I could play at any college in the nation, and if I wanted a shot at the NFL, all I had to do was work on my hang time. These performances, accolades, and words of encouragement, especially from touted athletes, were enough for me to keep all of my eggs in the football basket. Largely inspired by the notion of the American dream, I truly believed that everything would eventually work out for me, and that I would be lacing up on Sundays. I had imbibed that rugged American individualism, largely from television and movies — the notion that if you try hard enough and dream big enough, everything will work out in the end.

With this mindset, I took my talents and tried out for the football team at Northwest Missouri State University, a Division II powerhouse located in Maryville, Missouri. Thanks be to God, I was able to land a spot on the team as a walk-on and even start for the Bearcats my redshirt freshman year. The dream was continuing, and my subconscious mindset was, "No matter what, this will work." I can remember my long-snappers watching me warmup in practice and asking if I had an NFL leg. That was enough to keep those dreams dancing in my head. I believed that if I placed all of my eggs in the football basket, it would all work out — a naive idealism that God intended to purify and use later on in my life.

Let me switch gears here and talk about what was going on spiritually throughout these years. God planted seeds here and there in my life that would eventually blossom. Of course, the ultimate seed of divine life was planted on the day of my Baptism, when the Trinity entered into a new temple, a new Christian, thanks be to God!

Another major grace I received came from the priest who had administered my Baptism: Fr. James Flanagan. Father Flanagan, who passed away just recently — God rest his soul — was called by one writer "the most influential Catholic you have never heard of." His story is simply remarkable and made a huge impact, almost imperceptibly, on my life. He attended the University of Notre Dame on a football scholarship, cleared land mines from Normandy Beach preceding D-Day in World War II, became a member of the precursor to the Navy Seals, and then returned to Notre Dame and won three national football championships. After all that, he entered the seminary, became a priest, and founded a religious order, the Society of Our Lady of the Most Holy Trinity (SOLT). Talk about Hollywood material!

Father Flanagan's story became interwoven with mine because of the fact that, when my dad was in college, he got involved in missionary work in the Philippines. This is where he met Fr. Flanagan, who would eventually preside at my parents' wedding and baptize me and my little brother. I have seen video of Father entrusting a child he had just baptized to the Blessed Mother, and I believed he did the same with me.

My family still possesses a picture of Fr. Flanagan holding me in front of the tabernacle, presenting and entrusting me to the Eucharistic Lord. My dad would often share stories with me about Fr. Flanagan's saintly self-sacrifice, humor, and dedication to the priesthood. Every time my dad would share stories with me about Father, I felt something different — you could even say "otherworldly" — that drew me in. There was something that stuck out about those stories that, looking back now, I can only describe as the attraction of holiness. These stories were seeds being planted for a larger purpose that had yet to be revealed.

The next significant seeds would be planted during my high school years. My young theology teacher, Mr. Ringel, sought to impart the Catholic faith to us young people, a generation who, most of the time, were living in a different world, spiritually speaking. This made it difficult for Mr. Ringel to pass on what he knew in a way that would take hold in the souls of his students, because the faith has to be lived in order to be understood. Mr. Ringel's little sister Therese was in my class in grade school and high school, so I knew there was a commitment to the faith present in their family. This offered the same kind of attraction to holiness I had experienced with Fr. Flanagan.

Unfortunately, I became academically ineligible to play sports for my school during baseball season of my sophomore year. Mr. Ringel called me into his office and had a semi-disgusted and disappointed look on his face. I still remember what he said to me: "I thought you were smarter than this ... I asked my sister Therese about this, and she said you were too busy trying to be cool." Little did he know, but Mr. Ringel had pronounced a pithy diagnosis of my soul that would stick with me for many years and be a source of pain — in the good sense, because it would turn into a source of blessing. Out of all the corrections I had received in childhood and throughout high school, that one stuck with me so much, praise God.

As I pursued athletics in high school and college, my soul was plagued by a weakness that had been a byproduct of pursuing all the wrong things, following the wrong ideals, idolizing the wrong people, and caring way too much about what other people thought. The attraction to being known, the attraction to fitting in, the attraction to being worshipped in some sense was too much for my soul to fight, so I gave in. Once again, Mr. Ringel's diagnosis of "trying to be cool" could have rightly been branded on my arm at this time. This would manifest itself by falling into bad situations and patterns of behavior during high school, getting involved in alcohol, girls, and the party lifestyle, where responsibilities were shirked and all that mattered was fitting in and feeling good. I thought I could float by and live in these two worlds of sports and partying, and that somehow it would all work out. Little did I know sports and partying was all a mask hiding that I was neglecting the one relationship for which I was truly made.

Entering college, along with pursuing my punting career, helped cause my downward spiral into the party lifestyle — the lifestyle of fitting into the all-too-common narrative of college life shared by nearly every other student around me. If you don't think about it critically, you might just assume this was an inevitable part of the narrative of every young man's life, and that it would eventually pass. As I moved forward in college, God would start to let eggs fall out of the basket in which I had placed everything. Even though these experiences were painful at the time, He was using them to lead me towards Him.

During my redshirt freshman year, even after I had earned a starting spot on a very good college football team, my preparation, fitness, focus, and determination were nowhere to be found. Instead, I fell into the mindset of believing, "All I do is kick a ball." This was easy enough, and it gave me license to fall more and more into the party lifestyle. Then things took a turn for the worse: During the season, I was suspended for one game after receiving a citation for drinking alcohol while underage. Needless to say, my coach was not happy and I was ashamed. Some friends from high school had come up to watch me play that week, but I couldn't muster up the courage to tell them that I wasn't playing until after they had arrived.

Then more problems came. I fumbled a few snaps during the season, even one in a playoff game. As the team moved on to the National Championship game, I watched from the sidelines. That was probably the most scrutiny I had ever faced. It was definitely the most disappointment I had ever experienced. Those dreams in which I had so heavily invested myself looked as if they were starting to dry up. This would only give me more reasons to continue masking my problems, my distance from God, and my interior loneliness with created things. I quit Northwest Missouri's team after one year of play and thought about what my next plan of action would be.

It is so true that God works in mysterious ways. After I quit the football team, I started to have a serious desire to get away from the lifestyle that I had fallen into off the field. However, not content to let the dream of being an

All-American football hero die, I decided that I would transfer to the University of Missouri for a change of scenery and to get away from the pain of a failed freshman year. I would also give punting another shot as I pursued a walk-on position with Missouri's team. By the grace of God, I was granted a position on the team. The punter in front of me could not be beaten, but he would be graduating the next year, leaving an opening for me. Once again, the dream was kept alive, but, sadly, so were all of the bad partying habits I had accumulated, as well.

The emptiness grew. Not only did I lack any sense of purpose away from the field, but I was downright bewildered, plagued by the questions and suggestions of "Who had I become?" and "You were raised better than this." After a spring and summer training with the team, finally realizing that I was going nowhere fast, I decided to quit football and let the dream die. The sense of bewilderment grew, and I can honestly say that was one of the hardest experiences of my life up to that point. The self-doubt, disappointment, and sense that I had let everyone down, especially my parents, grew in a legion-like way. All of the expectations, false promises, and hopes placed in things that could never fulfill me evaporated like a mist. I realized there was nothing there.

This ultimately propelled me to go even deeper into masking the meaninglessness I perceived all around me. Now I was stuck in college without a purpose, in a major that I really had no interest in, and with what I perceived as superficial relationships with those friends closest to me. As this meaninglessness grew, a cry would grow in my soul, a cry for God, a cry to a Woman — the Woman — and boy, am I glad that they answered.

By the grace of God, EWTN was built into the cable package in the apartment complex I moved into during my junior year at Missouri. Thanks be to God for Mother Angelica of happy memory; her network was a Godsend. Many graces came to me (and still do) through that network's programming. I watched Venerable Fulton Sheen talking about how hard it is to come out of habitual sin. It was like he was speaking to my soul directly. My eyes began to be opened. It was scary because I realized that I was steeped in serious sin, and it became real to me that if I were to die in that state, I could go to hell forever. God had granted me light in my darkest time. I experienced an intense servile fear of the Lord, the fear of eternal damnation.

The awareness of my spiritual emptiness grew. I realized how far I was from God. I had drifted from going to Mass and realized that I had probably never made a serious Confession in all of my life up to that point. However, EWTN was a serious boon for me as I went through this time, a time where I didn't know who I was going to relate my spiritual experience to. I mean, who else could relate? One day, I heard the Divine Mercy Chaplet being sung on TV. I didn't know what it was at the time. All I remember was that it felt safe. I laid on my bed, face down, and just took it in as it was recited, like a child clinging to a security blanket. Another time of grace came when I saw the broadcast of Pope Benedict XVI on his visit to New York. As all the young people gathered around our Holy Father, cheering madly and rejoicing with him, tears came to my eyes. Once again, I sensed the attractive power of holiness, and I knew that I needed it.

As this all continued to come to a head, I experienced severe temptations to despair, self-hate, and loathing. In hindsight, it feels like the enemy, perhaps sensing that I was moving towards the light, intensified his efforts to end my life with God before it ever really began. One thing emphasized to me in my newfound catechesis was that if you are in trouble, you should call out to Our Blessed Mother. You have to take up the Rosary and cry out to her. I cried out to our Mother — albeit weakly. One time I tried to recite five decades of the Rosary, and I remember feeling so bewildered and confused while struggling to pray it that I could barely get one decade out. Yet I believe she heard the cry of her weak son. She came to help me, and that's when my journey home began.

One day, I reached a breaking point and felt mysteriously guided by the providence of God. I found my way to the confessional at the Newman Center on the University of Missouri's campus. Not even knowing what a general Confession was, I nonetheless made one. I poured out everything that had gone on in my soul — everything that I could possibly remember. The tears flowed. I was bawling. When I looked up, I saw that the priest was shedding tears as well. What a beautiful experience of God's mercy that was! In the midst of my tears and having no idea at all even to this day why, I yelled out, "I'm ready to do God's work." I have no idea why that came out of me at the time. I mean, that was the first real confession of my life, and now I'm ready to do God's work? The instrument of God's mercy — the Dominican priest in the confessional at the time — was so great. He reassured me that God had used great sinners and weak instruments such as St. Paul to accomplish His works. This was exactly what I needed to hear.

When I came out of the confessional that day, I kid you not, I saw reality in a different way. There had been spiritual scales taken off my eyes. Even physically, visually, it seemed that colors were brighter and that everything was glowing. The most dramatic piece out of all of this "spiritual candy" was the fact that I knew that I was loved by the Father, Son, and Holy Spirit. God was real. It was all real. I felt wrapped in the arms of the Heavenly Father, and I never wanted to leave. It was one of the greatest days of my life. I felt as though 2,000 pounds of spiritual weight had been cast off my shoulders.

Little did I know at the time that, even though I was completely forgiven in the confessional, those bad habits I had accumulated took a toll on my already-fallen nature and would be seriously hard to break. For about the next year and a half, I felt like I was two people. The old man and the new man were engaged in a serious struggle for my soul, and at times, I felt like I was going to break.

I fell back into old, bad habits. I was at an all-time new low, putting on weight and not seeing where my life was going. At the same time, I remember trying to go to Eucharistic

Adoration. The first time I got there, I wondered what everyone was looking at. Then it finally clicked — when we look at the Eucharist, we are not looking at an "it"; we are looking at Him, the Almighty. During this time, I also tried to attend daily Mass a few days each week when I could sneak over there between classes. Needless to say, my soul was in a dilemma that I didn't know how to escape.

Finally, I graduated from college in December of 2008 with a bachelor's degree in communications. Yes, it was an accomplishment, but I honestly had no idea where I was going. I even remember crying in the car on the way home from college with my dad because I still felt that emptiness, that meaninglessness. My soul was seriously torn in two and I didn't see it being put back together any time soon. In Kansas City, I linked back up with my old friends and went back to the ways of the world, all the while feeling totally empty and knowing that what I was doing was seriously wrong. I no longer enjoyed any of it, and I remember feeling numb, surrounding myself with created things and superficial people in order to mask what was going on deep down.

One night, my mom, Kathleen, and I were helping my sister move out of her old place, and I told my mom that I needed help, and that I needed her to help me. Even when I was messing up big time, when things were spiraling out of control, my mom was always there for me. She and my dad gave me unconditional love, even when I didn't deserve it; I saw God's face in them then, and I continue to see it. What a precious gift a mother's love is! Her self-sacrifice, her love, even when I didn't deserve it, is a living sign of God's love and something for which I will always be thankful. No words can articulate or repay all that she has done for me. I ask God daily to reward both of my parents as only He can.

As Lent of 2009 approached, and as the dichotomy in my soul intensified, I knew that I had to make a break for it or I might never get out my bad habits; that was the serious and intense grace that I received. On Ash Wednesday, I went with one of my best friends to Mass. He dropped me off at home and, even though he wasn't aware of it, I knew that he would not see me for a while.

After I got home that day, I was granted an amazing and firm resolve to really live the 40 days of Lent. Communication with my old friends was completely cut off. I turned off my phone and committed myself to saying the Rosary every single day. I also started going to daily Mass and occasional Adoration. It was an intense and beautiful time of grace in which serious spiritual chains that take some people years, and even a lifetime, to break, dramatically fell from me. The only times I left my parents' house during that Lent were to go to the gym or to Mass. During those 40 days, I was spiritually cleansed.

What started as a daily Rosary turned into two to three hours of daily prayer, mostly devotional. I remember discovering prayer to the saints, and especially prayer to the holy angels. During those 40 days, I felt freer than I ever had. I lost about 20 pounds from intense workouts and clean living. I was never a morning person, but during those days I would wake up with joy and praise God as I literally ran to the car to get to my workout and then, later in the morning, to Mass. Needless to say, God came into my life in a powerful and dramatic way.

I have to attribute a huge part of the grace given during that time to the power of the Rosary and the intercession of the Blessed Mother. I was consuming all the teachings of the Church, through the guidance of Mary. When I started to attend daily Mass during Lent, it was at the Redemptorist Church of Our Lady of Perpetual Help. Never has a truer title been given to Our Lady, because she gave me perpetual help at that time (and she still does). I have to stress to all: If you are searching for the Lord, go to His Mother. She will bring you to meet Him, and He will dine with you. *Totus Tuus Ego Sum Maria*!

After those 40 days of Lent were over, I still didn't know specifically where God was calling me. I only knew that, wherever it was, it would be with Him and His Holy Mother. In light of all the graces I had received, with an intense sense that we were engaged in a spiritual war, and that our Mother was gathering her troops, I realized that many of my family and friends were not seeing reality the same way. The world, the flesh, and the devil are strong, and I realized that my concern for souls was an intense gift from God. As I was sharing this with a priest in Confession, he asked me if I had ever thought about the priesthood. With full honesty, I can say that, up to that point, the priesthood wasn't really on my radar at all. But once again, the grace of God struck, and I realized after that question was asked that the priesthood was the path for me. God had implanted in my soul an intense burning desire for the salvation of souls and a desire to go forth under the mantle of the Blessed Mother to fight in the front lines of the great spiritual battle raging in our times.

When I first shared the news with my mother and father that I was now considering the priesthood, I think it was shocking to them. After all, no one could have predicted this even six months before. As we learned more and I talked with them and the local vocations director, Fr. Richard Rocha, about this decision, all the doors were opened. Father Richard Rocha was a former football player and coach [see Chapter 8], so it was the perfect fit. God took all those desires and gifts that He had given me for athletics and the football field to Himself and purified them, which He still continues to do. That same fall, only eight months after graduating from college without a clue, I would enter St. Gregory the Great Seminary in Seward, Nebraska, as a pre-theologian.

During those six years of seminary, my love for God, His Mother, and the priesthood grew, intensified, and crystallized. By the time I was in my second year of theology, I had received the grace of surety about my vocation to the priesthood. This was the path for me, and I pursued it full-bore. I formed relationships in the seminary that were deeper and more authentic than anything I had known before. They were rooted in Christ and a shared love for His Holy Mother. That's how a relationship lasts forever. I thoroughly enjoyed my time in seminary and pursued my studies and responsibilities with fervor (always in need of purification, however). I must also give thanks for all of those priests, religious sisters, lay professors, and dedicated lay people who supported and assisted my vocation. May God reward them all abundantly!

I was ordained as part of a class of 10 men for the Diocese of Kansas City-St. Joseph, Missouri, in May 2015. It was the greatest day of my life to that point. I still pinch myself and am astonished that I am now a priest of Jesus Christ. I hope I never lose this amazement at what God has done in me, with the assistance of our Holy Mother, the angels and saints, and my loved ones. *Laus Deo*!

After my ordination reception and when first blessings were over, I took a short visit to the Church of Our Lady of Perpetual Help — the place where I had begun attending daily Mass on a regular basis. I gave thanks to almighty God for the grace of the priesthood and poured out my love to my Mother for all of her tender care. She is beautiful, and she is with me every day.

Father Lickteig with his parents, Kathleen and Martin

Our Blessed Mother has been watching over me since my Baptism. She came for me, rescued me, and helped me go up to the sacred altar of God. I know that her assistance will never be lacking as we move forward in the great spiritual battle of our times. Get close to your Mother; pray your Rosary before the day is out. "No beads, no bed."

As I got closer to the altar, I realized that I had never met Fr. Flanagan as an adult. Over the course of my years in seminary, I had wanted at some point to go out to thank him and imbibe some of his priestly wisdom. This visit never materialized, but about a month before I was ordained to the priesthood, I was able to finally talk with Fr. Flanagan over the phone. I was informed before the call that he didn't see too well and that he was being cared for, yet I would have never guessed it from speaking with him.

As I told him who I was and that I was about to be ordained, he told me several times he was "overjoyed." His excitement was bursting through the phone. I could sense more life in the voice of that 90-year-old priest than I had heard in many younger ones before. I thanked him for all he had done for me, and he spoke about the priesthood and Our Lady. He told me to "ask her for whatever you want." Finally, I kneeled down as he gave me his priestly blessing through the phone, which lasted for a couple grace-filled minutes. It had all come full-circle. He told me to call him back after I was ordained so we could further talk about the priesthood. God willing, we will continue our conversation in Heaven someday.

As I look back over my life, over being in the priesthood for more than a year now, and as I grow into this exalted vocation, I know that even though I am a weak and worthless servant, the assistance of the Divine Mercy of the Lord, His Blessed Mother, the angels, and the saints will never be lacking. So I've seen and experienced firsthand that we have a Father who loves us intensely; that we have a Savior, Jesus Christ, whose Sacred Heart is burning for us in the tabernacle, in the Most Holy Eucharist. He wants us to turn to His Mercy with utmost confidence in His goodness, and He will shield us "as the hen doth gather her chickens under her wings."[1] The Holy Spirit will lead us, strengthen us, guide us, and sustain us if we give our will over to His guidance, and He will guide us with

---

[1] Mt 23:37

His spouse, our Holy Mother. Finally, I have to give a shout out to four very important people: Michael, Gabriel, Raphael, and my guardian angel, who have protected me over all these years on my journey back to God and to His altar. The angels are real, and we need to invoke their assistance every day!

Throughout my time in seminary and even now in the priesthood, I am very committed to staying in good physical shape, using exercise as a means to purify and sacrifice so the Lord can continue to use all of my humanity. God took all of my desires and talents and purified them from the false idols I had made of them. He took the desire to be cool and transformed it into a desire to be His fool, for God's wisdom looks like foolishness to many in our secularized world. God granted me true vision to see that the greatest in this world are the least, and that He sees the heart. You don't have to be validated by the world in order to be great; all you have to do is be "humbled therefore under the mighty hand of God, that he may exalt you in the time of visitation."[2] The glory of the athletic field always has to point to a greater prize, the ultimate prize, the eternal prize of life lived with the Father, Son, and Holy Spirit, with the Blessed Mother, the angels and saints, and all those who have attained the "never-fading crown of glory."[3]

I should offer a disclaimer that I in no way intend to disparage professional athletes or imply that they cannot be faithful: I know there are many faithful athletes out there. All I'm saying is that I know that if I had continued on the path I was on, I would most likely be going to perdition. Praise God that He came down in His mercy and showed me the way to train, to fight, to run the race towards the ultimate prize — the direct vision of Him.

Recently when I was at a young men's camp helping out as a priest, word got out that I used to kick. They had some light-up footballs for me to punt. I can still kick well enough to have little kids ask me if I ever thought about the NFL. My answer? "Yes, but Heaven is better." Amen.

[2] 1 Pet 5:6

[3] 1 Pet 5:4

FATHER
THOMAS HAAN

*Passing Along the
Catholic Faith*

My first love

During the opening credits of the iconic movie *Hoosiers*, newly-minted coach Norman Dale (played by Gene Hackman) navigates his vehicle through the gorgeous heartland of America, passing misty pastures, country churches, and sleepy grain elevators. He's headed to his new gig at Hickory High School, and as he approaches town on that peaceful fall morning, he spots two farm kids playing basketball on a hoop nailed to the side of their barn. This brief glance in the early moments of the film is intended to indicate the state of Indiana's near obsession with the game of basketball.

Director David Anspaugh never gave our family a call to have our farm be one of those depicted in the first minutes of his movie, but he could have. I learned to play the game of basketball (and came to love the game) on a seven-foot hoop in the hayloft of our family's barn. Sure, it was sweltering up there in the summer, but in the wintertime, an excuse was never needed to work on jump shots. My older brother, Paul, and I would have one-on-one battles late into the night. If that wasn't enough, my grandfather had a 10-foot hoop in *his* hayloft, complete with a painted "key" and free throw line. After we would sweep the loose hay and straw from the court, we'd have to look out for the occasional nail that had reared its head from the wooden floor. Two uncles had similar set-ups in their barns, which meant every family get-together involved 3-on-3, knockout, or a few rounds of "HORSE." Once we were thoroughly exhausted, we'd turn on the television to watch the likes of Larry Bird, Glenn Robinson, and Reggie Miller with awe. That fascination with basketball paid off in the end: My brother and I were able to live our own version of *Hoosiers*, being a part of our high school's 2003 Class A State Championship team.

A new love

It wasn't until junior high that other sports entered the picture for me. (Wasn't basketball all that mattered in Indiana?) I gave tackle football a try in seventh grade as a tight end, but on the opening kickoff of the second game of the season, a simple cut to the right resulted in a torn ACL (anterior cruciate ligament), MCL (medial collateral ligament), and torn cartilage in my left knee. Since I was still growing, I would have to sit out sports for the next year and a half to wait for surgery. In light of this disappointing experience, I was inclined to leave football for good. In the meantime, Paul had developed into an all-conference wide receiver and would go on to play for Indiana University. He wanted to practice catching the football in the front yard of our family farm, so he would constantly beg me to throw at him as hard as I possibly could. All of a sudden, football was fun again! It was Paul who noticed that I was developing a strong left arm (I'm a southpaw) and some serious accuracy, and it was Paul who stealthily gave a tip to the high school's head coach that I should try out for quarterback.

Thus commenced a six-year slew of skills camps, grueling two-a-day practices, private workouts, and endless throws to receivers. Strengthening my arm, working on precise timing and accuracy, getting quicker in my drop-back, reading defensive coverages, and getting physically stronger became my daily project. It was near the conclusion of my first full season of football as the junior varsity quarterback that I gradually became aware that I had more potential in football than in basketball, my first love in sports, and that God had given me more talent than most at the quarterback position.

I won the starting quarterback job for varsity my sophomore year, which meant throwing post-routes and fades to my brother, who by then was a senior occupied with breaking school receiving records. My family gushed with pride when the announcer would excitedly proclaim over the speakers, over and over again, "Haan completes the pass to Haan! First down!" If that wasn't enough, I had two cousins playing on the offensive line, so we were well represented.

By the time my senior year rolled around, our team had become known as an offensive juggernaut. We would average over 300 yards of passing a game, and by the end of the season, I would throw 41 touchdowns and just 10 interceptions. Though I had found my way into the state record books, I was from a small Catholic school, and at 6'1", I wasn't a "blue chip" recruit. What would I do for college? It would be a dream come true to play at the University of Notre Dame, to throw touchdowns in the House that Rockne built. But the Fighting Irish weren't recruiting me, nor were any of the other major schools in the area.

One day, I received a call that changed everything. Although Purdue University couldn't offer me a scholarship, they said I had a spot on the team for fall camp as an invited walk-on quarterback. Not only was Purdue the hometown school and the team I had grown up watching, but it was the "Cradle of Quarterbacks," the collegiate home of Bob Griese, Len Dawson, Mike Phipps, Gary Danielsen, Mark Herrmann,

Jim Everett, Drew Brees, and Kyle Orton. I was going to be a Boilermaker!

My tenure on the Purdue football team was at one and the same time a glorious dream and a constant struggle, a thrill and a whirlwind, an honor and a reality check. In the end, it only lasted a year, but it was an experience of a lifetime. It was such a brief and unremarkable collegiate career statistically, but unforgettable and formative. Every time I watch the movie "Rudy" (which is more frequently than I'd like to admit), I sympathize with the protagonist in his daily struggle to prove himself to the coaches against the game's elite. As an invited walk-on, it felt as though I got less chances, less looks from the coaches, and in many ways, that's probably true. Sometimes I became discouraged and doubted my abilities, but many times, it caused me to increase my effort, intensity, and commitment. Beyond my family, my support included many of my teammates, who respected how hard I worked and how I studied the game. Fellow players became close friends and great sources of encouragement.

Not all teammates provided support, though. Even though the team was loaded with NFL talent, the 2005 Boilermakers were the first squad led by Coach Joe Tiller that didn't qualify for a bowl game. Without a doubt, this disappointing season was caused primarily by a group of selfish players who were more concerned about their professional futures than their collegiate present. I would see them talk back to coaches, give half-effort at practice, and blow off younger members of the team. In the locker room, I would overhear them bragging of their exploits with women, using them as objects, tossing them aside, and laughing about it. Their attitude about life and their approach to being a teammate was a clear warning to me: Selfishness is cancerous to a team.

I spent that very mediocre season working on the scout team each week, mimicking the plays that the upcoming opponent would probably run, in order to prepare the first-string defense for that week's game. It was often a thankless job. When I did well and made a great throw, the coaches would get mad at the *defense*; if I made a mistake such as making the wrong throw or running the wrong play, the coaches would get mad at *me* for wasting their time. Although it was our job to prepare them, the scout team rejoiced any time we would score against the starters.

After winter conditioning, spring practices, and a brief appearance in the Spring Game, I sat down with our new quarterbacks coach, where we both agreed that with the recruits coming on campus that fall, it would be nearly impossible for me to make any progress on the depth chart. It became clear that achieving my personal goals as an athlete would be impossible at Purdue. I had a huge decision in front of me: Do I transfer to a smaller school to achieve my goals, or is it time to re-examine those goals and look at the big picture of my life? Where am I headed, and where does God want to lead me?

A divine love

Frequently I am asked when I became aware of God's call to the priesthood. Did I know while I was shooting hoops in the barn? While I was calling plays in the huddle? For some, the call is dramatic and sudden, unmistakable and even thrilling. My own story, on the other hand, is one of a gradual unfolding, a series of experiences that culminated in certainty by the time I graduated college. I grew up in a loving, faith-filled home. My dad and mom taught us kids how to pray, would take us to Mass every Sunday (no matter what), and would even occasionally read us daily devotionals before school. We would eat dinner together as a family nearly every night, but the priesthood was never really brought up as an option in conversation. Throughout high school, I can't say I gave the priesthood a serious thought. I dated a girl for a couple of years, and had just assumed marriage was what God had planned for me. Sure, I probably spent more time in prayer than my peers, but that wasn't so weird, was it? I would privately slip into our town's perpetual adoration chapel after our football and basketball games, but I didn't see that as odd.

A crucial factor in my gradual awareness of a vocation was my relationship with our parish priest. Through high school and college, he was for me both a resource of spiritual wisdom and a model of a joy-filled priest. We would regularly meet to discuss the spiritual life and how I could offer my athletic efforts to the glory of God. He would have me read the writings of St. Thérèse of Lisieux and St. John Paul II, and would ask me, "Are you open to whatever God has in store for you?" Those conversations led to a deepened love for our Lord, and a greater yearning to live for Him and Him alone. I didn't know exactly what God had in store, but I was ready for whatever He would ask of me.

At the end of my year on the Purdue football team, I decided not to transfer, but to remain as a student, and would help coach a junior high football team at my alma mater. Oddly enough, it was while working with those pimply, awkward 13- and 14-year-olds that my vocational inclinations became more pronounced! On those sidelines, I realized that, while I enjoyed teaching them the mechanics of throwing a spiral and the footwork of a five-step drop, what I *really* cared about was their growth in virtue, in faith, and in holiness. I began to ask myself, "Should I do something that involves those concerns full-time?"

Meanwhile, I had discovered a discernment program for undergraduate men run by the Congregation of Holy Cross at the University of Notre Dame, and it seemed like the perfect fit: going to morning prayer and daily Mass in a house of similarly discerning men, discussing the spiritual life and the call to the priesthood. It wouldn't be a total commitment to the priesthood, but it would be a step in that direction. And I would still be able to attend football games on Saturdays at Notre Dame Stadium. I decided to transfer to South Bend for the final two years of undergraduate study, confident that it was in the land of Touchdown Jesus, the Grotto, and the Basilica of the Sacred Heart that I would discover my vocation, whether it was to the priesthood or not.

Though I had put my collegiate football dreams behind me, my ache for intense competition remained while at Notre Dame. At the encouragement of some friends, I joined the school's amateur boxing team, whose pinnacle event is the famed "Bengal Bouts" tournament each spring. This was an exhilaration unlike any other, and through boxing, I got into the best shape of my life. The focus on technique and strategy helped me understand why boxing is known as the "sweet science." I made it all the way to the semifinals in my weight class, and had a Jesuit priest giving me advice and encouragement as my "corner man" in the ring! A cheering section of Holy Cross seminarians at a boxing tournament was certainly memorable.

As I drew near graduation and was struggling to arrive at certainty about my own vocation, a conversation with a campus priest provided great insight. In an effort to clarify my discernment, I was driving myself crazy by imagining two future scenarios, hoping that a spiritual joy would overcome me while contemplating one or the other: being a priest at a parish, or being married with a wife, kids, a job, and a home of my own. The priest sagely told me to stop the endless, futuristic joy-searching, and ponder what was bringing about the most profound joy for me on a regular basis *now*, as a student. Without skipping a beat, I told him that it was when I could assist someone in drawing nearer to the person of Jesus Christ that I was regularly filled with authentic joy. The veteran priest silently smirked at me, leading me to confront the reality that God created me to lead souls to Christ, and that's exactly what a priest does, day in and day out. The answer to the question of my vocation finally dawned on me. Would it be difficult not having a wife? A life of freedom? Owning a home? Of course! But these brief glimpses of joy were indications that our Lord would satisfy every desire of my heart. There was good reason to trust Him, so I decided I would enter major seminary in the fall, where I would study theology and be formed for the priesthood.

Love of sports remains

While studying theology at Mount St. Mary's Seminary in Emmitsburg, Maryland, I certainly did *not* leave sports behind. I joined the seminary's intramural basketball and flag football teams, which competed against university students, and I would participate in team triathlons and 5k charity races. I was even asked to be the chaplain of the university's men's lacrosse team for three years. We seminarians would gather in the rec room to watch the big sporting events, each man rooting on his favorite team. Much like teammates, seminarians enjoy a true brotherhood, and that brotherhood endures in the fraternity of the Catholic priesthood.

It is humbling to know that God has decided to con-figure me to Christ the High Priest and calls me to act *in persona Christi*, but, since my priestly ordination in 2013, I have become convinced of the grace God provides me to live my vocation as a spiritual father. As Fr. Lacordaire wrote in his beautiful poem about the priesthood, I "go from men to God/and offer Him their prayers;/to return from God to men/to bring pardon and hope … .'" It is one thing to have a theological grasp of the reality of the sacramental priesthood, but it is entirely another thing to have the experience of living the priesthood in light of that reality. I often say the priesthood gives me a front row seat to God's grace in action. Whether it be seeing God's mercy in the context of the confessional or seeing His self-giving love in the Eucharist, the priesthood is filled with extraordinary moments.

I now find myself a chaplain at Guerin Catholic High School in Noblesville, Indiana, teaching theology, offering the sacrifice of the Mass each day, hearing confessions, and giving spiritual direction. It's not unlike my former role as a quar-terback. Just as a quarterback needs to know each offensive player's assignment, to read the attack of the defense and to encourage the team to success through word and example, the priest must know the valuable and unique role of each mem-ber of his flock. He must see the potential dangers and errors in our culture that threaten to inhibit the Church's progress toward its goal. It is the priest's task to lead souls to Heaven by word and example. While at the high school, I make it a point to be present at the sporting events of all of our student athletes. It is my vocation to bear witness to the reality that the ultimate goal is sainthood and eternal communion with God, and that sports are merely a means to that end, not an end in itself.

On the occasions I am able to have a day away from the school, I'll head back to see my parents and help out on the farm. As I drive past the wide expanse of Hoosier cornfields and pastures, I sometimes see youngsters tossing a football around in their front yard, and I'm tempted to join them. As I'm stacking hay bales in the barn with my dad, I resist the urge to stop and put up a jump shot. No, the competitive drive hasn't left me, nor has my love for sports, but a more profound love has captivated me and led me to a life driven by a thirst for souls. My ache for competition has succumbed to a yearning for God, and I'm so thankful that He has invited me to be a Catholic priest, and to awaken that same yearning in others.

AFTERWORD
by Eric Mahl

Just one thing: forgetting what lies behind but
straining forward to what lies ahead, I continue
my pursuit toward the goal, the prize of
God's upward calling, in Christ Jesus.

— Philippians 3:13-14

ISOUGHT TO DO JUST THIS WHEN I answered my
call to follow God, not only away from football, but to
live as a hermit alone with the Bible for three years and then
to go out into the streets to live as a homeless man in order
to bring the love of Jesus to the poor. No one cared that I
was the strongest athlete in the history of my university when
I lived in a hermitage; no one knew that I was a former NFL
linebacker as I lived on the street as a homeless man. I had
only one focus: Jesus Christ. I forgot what was behind me
and "strained forward" to the ultimate "prize," not a trophy
that will rust, but Christ Jesus in whom I will abide forever.
In this new life, everything I ate, drank, and did was now for
the glory of God. I was now driven, not to be the best, but to
be a child of God. When you encounter the living God, your
entire world will be turned upside down.

In 2002, St. John Paul II proclaimed to the youth of the
world:

It is the nature of human beings, and especially
youth, to seek the Absolute, the meaning and fullness of life. Dear young people, do not be content

with anything less than the highest ideals! Do not let yourselves be dispirited by those who are disillusioned with life and have grown deaf to the deepest and most authentic desires of their heart. You are right to be disappointed with hollow entertainment and passing fads, and with aiming at too little in life.

So I ask you: What is this ideal? What is your highest ideal? Or rather, *who* is this highest ideal? This is what humanity has been searching for since the foundation of the world. We long to find what makes us fully alive, what brings us utter happiness, what gives us the sense of purpose we need in order to give our lives to something great. We long to know why we exist and why we are here in this world.

The great majority of the world's population has at one point in their lives thought that it was sports that bring the greatest happiness, the greatest joy, and the purpose of their lives. So many think that being a part of a sports team or even a fan of a particular team fulfills our deep longing for community.

These 11 men whose stories you've discovered in *Apostolic Athletes* give us the correct answer. It is only in Jesus Christ that we find our purpose. It is only in Jesus Christ that we become fully alive. And it is only in Jesus Christ that our joy will ultimately be found, because He came to bring that joy abundantly (see Jn 15:11). These 11 men have found that the team they searched for was not one wearing particular colors or jerseys, but rather the community of the Mystical Body of Christ. Here in this book, you have found men who were not "content with anything less than the highest ideals." Once they found the Highest Ideal, they gave their entire lives to it. That refusal to settle for less than the best propelled them to climb the steps to the altar. Now the sacrifice they offer for their team is not eating a bland protein diet, nor early morning workouts, nor the dreaded two-a-day practices under the scorching August sun. The sacrifice they offer is the Body, Blood, Soul, and Divinity of Jesus Christ in the Eucharist.

... whatever gains I had, these I have come to consider a loss because of Christ. More than that, I even
consider everything as a loss because of the supreme
good of knowing Christ Jesus my Lord. For his sake
I have accepted the loss of all things and I consider
them so much rubbish, that I may gain Christ (Phil
3:7-8).

For many years of my life, these words from Scripture
matched a desire of my heart. I knew that by walking away
from the game of football, I was losing a great part of my life
where sports were the priority; where everything I ate, drank,
and did served one purpose: to make me the best football
player on the field. Athletics were all-consuming for me. I felt
the drive to reach greatness in everything I did in the athletic
world. Well, except for one thing, the most important thing,
the one thing that would never be taken away (see Lk 10:42):
my relationship with God, which was lukewarm at best. My
identity was as an athlete first, and somewhere down the line
was my love for God and His children.

The Lord calls us to humility, gentleness, and a complete
gift of self in love for our neighbors. I was proud, aggressive,
and believed the entire world revolved around me. But the
God that I began to encounter is a God of love who patiently
calls us and gives us time so that we may turn away from our
ways of sin and towards Him. Once we have the opportunity to
know Him as the God of Love, we begin to see who we most
truly, most deeply are — beloved children of God in Christ
Jesus (not athletes first and foremost). With these two key
insights into the truth about God and our identity in Christ,
we then begin to understand how we are called to reveal God
to the world, living as witnesses to the Gospel. Once we begin
to know our God, we cannot help but fall in love with Him. It
is then that we can no longer live solely for ourselves.

It was only recently that someone told me, "Eric, the only
reason someone would listen to you teach the Gospel is because
you played football." This was a very sobering statement that

I had to let sit for a while. But why? Do people listen to me talk about Jesus because I used to be bigger, faster, and stronger than them? Or do they listen to the message of Divine Mercy from my lips because I reached a level in the sports world that so few will ever attain? Maybe it is because I had an opportunity for the American Dream and intentionally chose Jesus Christ. Either way, I wanted to "forget" my past in sports, but the Lord uses everything in our lives to proclaim His Mercy — the good, the bad, and the ugly. All is His. I am beginning to understand this.

I never know why people listen to athletes when they give their lives to Christ. But what I do know is that they listen.

What you hold in your hand is a book containing the stories of athletes who have given their lives to Christ and His Church. Each of these men of God has a story about their life in Christ, about a journey that means they no longer identify as athletes first and followers of Christ second. These men are Apostolic Athletes. These men have been formed through their sports experiences and found that God was preparing them, teaching them, and now sends them out to proclaim the Gospel.

In the world we live in, we need witnesses who have chosen Jesus over everything the world has to offer, whose lives are as light in darkness, which leads us to give glory to God. In *Apostolic Athletes*, we have had the blessing to hear from such witnesses. Let their words inspire you on your own journey and your own call. Find in these stories the courage to hear God calling you to Himself, forming you in His Gospel, and sending you out to make "disciples of all nations." I encourage you to be inspired by this book to strive for nothing less than the highest ideal — Jesus Christ our Lord — and give Him your life.

FURTHER READING

Christ, the Ideal of the Priest by Blessed Columba Marmion (Ignatius Press, 2005)

Many Are Called by Scott Hahn (Doubleday, 2010)

Priesthood by Fr. Wilhelm Stockums (TAN Books/St. Benedict Press, 2009)

Sunday Sermons of St. Alphonsus Liguori by St. Alphonsus Liguori (TAN Books, 2009)

Tell My Priests by Fr. George Kosicki, CSB (Marian Press, 2012)

The Incredible Catholic Mass by Venerable Martin von Cochem (TAN Books, 1997)

The Priest: His Dignity and Obligations by St. John Eudes (Loreto Publications, 2008)

The Priest Is Not His Own by Venerable Fulton Sheen (Ignatius Press, 2004)

The Priest in Union with Christ by Fr. Reginald Garrigou-LaGrange, OP (TAN Books, 2002)

The Priest: Man of God by St. Joseph Cafasso (TAN Books, 2009)

The Spiritual Exercises of Saint Ignatius by St. Ignatius of Loyola (TAN Books, 2010)

Those Mysterious Priests by Venerable Fulton Sheen (St. Paul's/Alba House, 2005)

To Save a Thousand Souls by Fr. Brett Brannen (Vianney Vocations, 2010)

Under the Mantle by Fr. Donald Calloway, MIC (Marian Press, 2013)

Visits to the Blessed Sacrament by St. Alphonsus Liguori (TAN Books, 2001)